AYERS ROCK

By the same author

THE ART OF ALBERT NAMATJIRA
BROWN MEN AND RED SAND
THE ART, MYTH AND SYMBOLISM OF ARNHEM LAND
THE TIWI, THEIR ART, MYTH AND CEREMONY
ABORIGINAL ART
ABORIGINAL PAINTINGS FROM AUSTRALIA
THE DREAMTIME: Aboriginal Mythology in the Art of Ainslie Roberts

Aboriginal in initiation cave, Ayers Rock

AYERS ROCK

Its People, Their Beliefs and Their Art

CHARLES P. MOUNTFORD

EAST-WEST CENTER PRESS
HONOLULU

FIRST PUBLISHED IN 1965 BY ANGUS & ROBERTSON LTD, SYDNEY, MELBOURNE, LONDON

LIBRARY OF CONGRESS CATALOG CARD NO. 65-16798

PUBLISHED IN THE UNITED STATES BY EAST-WEST CENTER PRESS, HONOLULU

PRINTED IN AUSTRALIA BY HALSTEAD PRESS, SYDNEY

ACKNOWLEDGMENTS

OVER the long period I have been engaged on this research and the preparation of this book, I have been helped by many people. To all of these I offer my grateful thanks.

First, I must express thanks to my young friend, the late Mr L. E. Sheard, for his companionship on the 1940 expedition and his help when I attempted the time-consuming plan of recording the art of Ayers Rock by scale drawings.

I also owe much to the generosity of the late Miss Margaret Symon and Mrs Mary Clark, whose gift made it possible to continue my Ayers Rock research; to Lady Grenfell Price, who, through the University of Adelaide, provided the generous subsidy necessary for the publication of this book; and to the Honourable Paul Hasluck for his assistance.

I am also grateful to the Board of Governors and the Director of the South Australian Museum, Dr Peter Crowcroft, for the use of their facilities and the loan of the colour block of the Mutitjilda cave; to Mr Hedley Brideson, Principal Librarian of the Public Library, for his assistance in the preparation of the illustrations; to Mrs and Mr John Michell, the former for her watercolour of the totemic creatures of Ayers Rock and the latter for the gift of the colour block; to Dr Kenneth Oakley, of the British Museum of Natural History, for the loan of the block of my photograph used for the Frontispiece; to the Katatjuta Publishers, for the two colour blocks of Ayers Rock, and to Miss Brenda Hubbard for her watercolour of the cave paintings in the Mutitjilda cave.

To Professor G. H. Lawton and Dr C. R. Twidale I am particularly indebted for guiding my stumbling footsteps through the preparation of the M.A. thesis which forms the core of this book, and to Miss Margaret King, my daughter-in-law Mrs K. P. Mountford, and my wife, for their patient work in reading and editing the manuscript.

Without the unstinted and generous help of these folk and many others, the book would never have been completed.

CHARLES P. MOUNTFORD

25 First Avenue,
St Peters, South Australia.

CONTENTS

Acknowledgments v

Introduction xiii

Part One

THE PITJANDJARA AND THEIR LANDS

1 The Tribal Land 3

2 Hunting and Food-gathering Equipment 7

3 Means of Gaining a Livelihood in the Desert 13

4 The Tribal Organization 18

Part Two

THE BELIEFS OF THE PITJANDJARA

5 The Creation Beliefs 23

6 The Topography of Ayers Rock 27

7 The Myths of Ayers Rock 31

(a) The Carpet-snakes, Kunia, and the Venomous Snakes, Liru 31

(b) The Hare-wallabies, Mala, and the Spirit Dingo, Kulpunya 68

(c) The Lizard-men, Kandju and Linga 114

(d) The Marsupial Moles, Itjari-tjari 126

(e) The Man and Woman, Kadidi 132

(f) The Sleepy-lizard man, Meta-lungana 138

(g) The Willy-wagtail Woman, Tjinderi-tjinderiba 144

(h) The Mythical Snake, Wanambi 152

Part Three

THE ART OF AYERS ROCK

8 The Art of the Rock Engravings 157

9 The Art of the Sacred Objects 162

10 The Art of the Cave Paintings 175

Summary 197

Bibliography 201

Index 203

ILLUSTRATIONS

Colour Plates

Aboriginal in initiation cave, Ayers Rock	*Frontispiece*
Ayers Rock from the east	*Between pages* xiv and 1
Ayers Rock from the west	2 and 3
Totemic creatures at Ayers Rock	34 and 35
Cave paintings, Mutitjilda Gorge	178 and 179

Black and White Plates

1	Portraits, Pitjandjara Aborigines	6
2	Hunting and food-gathering equipment	11
3-4	Topography of Ayers Rock	28-29
5-10	Carpet-snakes, Kunia	34-39
11-14	Poisonous snakes, Liru	41-44
15-17	Carpet-snake woman, Bulari	45-47
18-19	Carpet-snakes, Kunia	48-49
20-1	Poisonous snakes, Liru	51-52
22-30	Carpet-snakes, Kunia	53-64
31-2	Hare-wallaby, Mala woman, and poisonous snake, Liru man	65-66
33-63	Hare-wallabies, Mala	67-103
64-6	Red-backed kingfisher-woman, Lunba	104-106
67-70	Spirit dingo, Kulpunya	107-111
71-2	Hare-wallabies, Mala	112-113
73-6	Lizard, Kandju	115-118
77-84	Lizard, Linga	119-128
85-9	Marsupial moles, Itjari-tjari	129-134
90-1	Man and woman, Kadidi	135-136
92-7	Sleepy-lizard, Meta-lungana	137-143

98-104	Willy-wagtail woman, Tjinderi-tjinderiba	145-153
105	Paintings in Mutitjilda Cave	179
106	Ceremonial decorations of the Pitjandjara	183

Figures in the Text

1.	Geographic position of Ayers Rock	xiii
2.	Hunting and food-gathering equipment	9
3.	Totemic map of Ayers Rock	32
4.	Rock engravings, Ayers Rock	159
5.	Rock engravings, Tiyin rockhole, Katatjuta	159
6.	Rock engravings, Wina rockhole, Katatjuta	160
7.	Rock engravings, Walpa Gorge, Katatjuta	161
	Figs 8-26. Sacred kulpidji	
8.	Camps of carpet-snakes, Kunia, at Ayers Rock	162
9.	Carpet-snakes, Kunia, women at Ayers Rock	163
10.	Venomous snake-men, Liru, travelling to Katatjuta (Mt Olga)	163
11.	Venomous snake-men, Liru, at Katatjuta (Mt Olga)	164
12.	Old Mala men asleep in their camps	164
13.	Mala men decorating themselves for ceremony	165
14.	Mala men and initiates at ceremony	165
15.	Naldawata pole at Mala initiation ceremony	166
16.	Mala women at Tabudja	166
17.	Old Mala man guarding women at Tabudja	167
18.	Mala women and children in their camp	167
19.	The Liru man and Mala woman	168
20.	Body of the spirit dingo, Kulpunya	168
21.	Journey of the spirit dingo, Kulpunya	169
22.	Kulpunya and the Mala women	169
23.	The lizard, Kandju, and his lost boomerang	170
24.	The marsupial mole, Itjari-tjari	170

25. The sleepy-lizard, Meta-lungana, and the emu meat 171
26. Motifs on *kulpidji* at Ayers Rock 172
FIGS 27-43. Cave paintings
27. Cave painting sites, Ayers Rock 177
28. Site 1 178
29. Site 1 180
30. Site 2 *between pages* 180-181
31. Site 3 181
32. Site 4 184
33. Site 5 185
34. Site 4 *between pages* 186-187
35. Site 6 186-187
36. Site 9 186-187
37. Site 7 186
38. Site 8 (upper) 187
39. Site 8 (lower) 188
40. Site 8 (lower) 189
41. Site 11 192
42. Site 12 193
43. Cave Paintings, Ayers Rock 194

INTRODUCTION

Ayers rock is an enormous monolith rising almost vertically for over eleven hundred feet from a level sandy desert which is more than one hundred miles across (Fig. 1). The sheer immensity of this great Rock in the middle of an extensive level plain, and its vivid colouring particularly towards morning and evening, makes it one of the wonders of Australia, if not of the world.

Fig. 1. Geographic position of Ayers Rock.

When, in 1935, I first visited the Rock, I was so impressed with its strange beauty and vast size that I set myself the task of making a survey of all phases of aboriginal life associated with this natural feature.

Since that first visit, I have made four attempts to complete that task, including several months spent journeying with the aboriginal men and women of the Pitjandjara tribe.

Although, as a result of the three earlier expeditions, I ascertained a general pattern of the daily life of the Pitjandjara people, as well as the myths and art of Ayers Rock, I did not feel that the material gathered, particularly on the latter subjects, was sufficiently detailed or accurate for publication.

The main reasons for this were—the inability to stay long enough at Ayers Rock to carry out extensive research; and the fact that my informants were not Ayers Rock men and, therefore, did not know the myths in detail, or they were men who, though belonging to the country, were too young when they left Ayers Rock to have gained a full knowledge of the myths, many of which belong to the secret life of the fully initiated men.

In 1960 another attempt was made, on this occasion with ample time to complete the task started twenty years earlier. As far as could be determined, there were few Ayers Rock men then living, and only one of them, Balinga, a *Mala* (hare-wallaby) man, having passed through all the rites of initiation at Ayers Rock, was therefore fully adult before he had left his tribal country.

From the results of my previous research I was able to judge that Balinga, who became my informant, was particularly well versed in the stories explaining the mythical origins of the topographical features of Ayers Rock. For this reason his statements have been used whenever they differed from those of earlier informants.

This book, as its title indicates, will deal with Ayers Rock and its people. Three aspects will be discussed: (*a*) the tribal country of the Pitjandjara, on the eastern boundary of which Ayers Rock, or to give it the aboriginal name, Uluru, is situated, the daily life of the men and women, and their means of gaining a livelihood in their inhospitable desert country; (*b*) the aborigines' conception of the creation of their world, and in particular the mythological origin of the topographical features of Ayers Rock; (*c*) a study of the graphic arts of Ayers Rock, the rock markings, the engravings on the sacred objects, and the paintings in the many caves around the base of the monolith.

In recent years the effects of civilization and the restrictive practices of the Christian missions have caused rapid changes to take place in the culture of the Pitjandjara tribe. Therefore, to make the description clearer, references will be made to their culture as it was when in 1940 I made a long camel journey, extending over some months, with the Pitjandjara men and women through their own country. At this time these people, almost untouched by external influences, were following their original way of life.

Ayers Rock from the east

Part One

THE PITJANDJARA AND THEIR LAND

Ayers Rock from the west

Chapter 1

THE TRIBAL LAND

THE boundaries of the tribal land of the Pitjandjara have never been satisfactorily determined. My own inquiries suggest that they extend from the southern flanks of the Musgrave Ranges northward to Lake Amadeus, eastward to the Basedow Ranges, and westward to the western limits of the Musgrave Ranges. The aborigines, however, do not look on their tribal land as a strictly limited area, but as a number of small clearly defined hunting territories, each of which is the home of a family group[1] and the aggregate of which forms the land of the Pitjandjara tribe.

The tribal land of the Pitjandjara is unusually arid, particularly as one leaves the Musgrave Ranges and travels northward. This area consists predominantly of parallel lines of drifting sandridges, the bare crests of which move, under the influence of the prevailing wind, along their length.

The sides of the sandridges are covered with spinifex and low shrubs, and the swales between with occasional stands of desert oaks, mulga and the ever-present spinifex.

The weather records of the desert are sparse and incomplete. Those taken in the Musgrave and Rawlinson Ranges show an average rainfall of eight inches a year, while a four-year record at Curtin Springs which, being in the open desert, is free from the influences of the ranges, is only five inches. This low rainfall, almost equally distributed throughout the year, coupled with high temperatures and a mean relative humidity of twenty-five per cent, has created a country of considerable aridity and limited water supplies, conditions which have determined the fauna and flora that can live in such an environment. The aborigines, too, have adapted themselves to live successfully in such a harsh and unfriendly country.

There is a widespread belief that the Australian aborigines are mentally inferior to the white man. Those who have had the happy experience of travelling and living with them, particularly if by

[1] These areas will be called the clan territories.

oneself, will have no doubt about the intelligence of his aboriginal companions. The skill which the Pitjandjara men and women employ in meeting the hazards of their life, in gaining a livelihood with their extremely limited food-gathering equipment, and their quick and intelligent responses when faced with an emergency, will soon convince the white visitor that his aboriginal companions have intelligent, well-trained minds quite equal in calibre to those of the average white man.

There is also an erroneous idea that the intellectual capacity of the members of a society can be judged by the number of tools they use to gain a livelihood, or, in other words, by the simplicity or otherwise of their material culture.

This idea is completely exploded when we examine the aborigines of the desert of central Australia, who, with only five simple tools (Fig. 2), are able to gain an adequate livelihood in an environment so arid that no white man could live in it unless he took food with him. For this fact alone, it must be admitted that they are intelligent people.

The desert aborigines, whose life is one of continuous movement from one waterhole to the next in their search for food, have learnt to gain a livelihood with a minimum of equipment. They are entirely mobile. Should a family move from one camping ground to another, the men have nothing to do but pick up their spears and spearthrowers and the women to put their carrying dishes on their heads and take their digging sticks in their hands; then, whether they are absent from that locality for days, weeks or months, they have all they need to gain a livelihood.

Anyone who has travelled with these people day after day, with no idea of exploiting them or of changing their way of life, will soon develop an esteem and often a considerable affection for them. From the many investigators who have spoken highly of their aboriginal guides and informants, I have chosen four.

Eyre (1845, p.155) wrote, "I do not imagine that his vices would usually be found greater, nor his passions more malignant than that of a very large proportion of men ordinarily considered civilized.... These people [aborigines] . . . on many occasions cheerfully underwent hunger, thirst and fatigue to serve me."

Gregory (1906, pp.179-80), speaking of his Deiri guides when he was exploring the Lake Eyre Basin, wrote, "I always felt toward them that they were men, or brothers. They have much quiet dignity and their humour, with regard to things in general, was like that of an intelligent, but untrained European."

Grey (1841, p.267) maintains that "they were as apt and intelligent as any other race that I am acquainted with".

Fry (1935, p.355), who spent many years investigating the mental characteristics of the aborigines of the desert, states, "He [the aboriginal] is normally light-hearted and cheerful. Parental feelings are strong; children are indulged and seldom punished. Filial devotion to aged parents is also strongly developed. Self-esteem and dignity are the perquisites of the old men who are learned in the tribal lore."

For thirty years I have spent many months with the desert aborigines, in particular with those of the Pitjandjara tribe. I cannot speak too highly of the many courtesies, the friendliness, and the help received from these desert people, and the pleasures enjoyed in their companionship, as far as companionship is possible between members of such widely differing cultures. I have always felt the same as Gregory: that they were men and brothers who did not serve me for a reward, but because they accepted me as a guest whom they were prepared to help in any way they could.

On Plate 2 are four desert aborigines who have been my companions for many weary miles; A, Moanya, stern and reticent, but always willing to instruct me in the lore of his people; B, Kamanalda, a particularly able and loyal companion on one of the most difficult journeys I ever undertook in central Australia; C, Jabiaba, a dignified, but merry soul, who was often surrounded by a group of laughing children; and D, Numidi, quick-witted and full of vitality and fun.

It is a memorable experience to have lived and travelled with these and other aborigines and to have been able to see, if only for a short time, the functioning of one of the most primitive cultures of mankind: a culture with tools so simple that the gaining of a livelihood in that desert environment is a remarkable achievement; a culture with a code of laws so well balanced that there is no need for organized warfare to maintain a social balance; and a culture where the people are at peace with each other and with the surroundings in which they live.

PLATE 1. Pitjandjara aborigines: A, Moanya; B, Kamanalda; C, Jabiaba; D, Numidi.

Chapter 2

HUNTING AND FOOD-GATHERING EQUIPMENT

THE hunting and food-gathering equipment (Fig. 2 and Pl. 2) with which the members of the Pitjandjara tribe gain a livelihood are simple and few in number. They are:

(i) Barbed, wooden, hunting spear.
(ii) Spearthrower.
(iii) Wooden carrying dish.
(iv) Digging stick.
(v) Upper and lower grinding stones.

(i) Hunting Spear (Fig. 2A)

The shaft of this spear, usually about ten feet long, is made up of several lengths of tecoma vine spliced together and bound with kangaroo sinews. The shaft has a leaf-shaped point of mulga with a recurved wooden barb, held in place by a mass of spinifex gum, and bound to the shaft with sinews. There is a shallow hole in the opposite end of the shaft to accommodate the throwing peg of the spearthrower.

(ii) Spearthrower (Fig. 2F)

The spearthrower of the Pitjandjara is a general purpose tool. It has four uses:

(*a*) As a spearthrower, which will enable the aborigines to cast the spear both farther and more accurately.[1]
(*b*) As a cutting tool. The adze stone, usually a flake of fine-grained quartzite, is mounted in spinifex gum on one end of the spearthrower. This tool is used for smoothing and shaping the spears and spearthrowers; cutting up the flesh of the creatures; putting the final finish on the wooden carrying dishes, and for other similar purposes.

[1] In a competition the Pitjandjara aborigines were able to cast a spear the maximum distance of 89 yards. They were not accurate, however, over a distance much greater than 20 yards. (Mountford, Field Notes, 1940.)

(*c*) As a dish. The hollow body of the spearthrower is used for holding food of various kinds, or the blood used as an adhesive to fasten the bird-down on the performers in the sacred rituals.
(*d*) For fire-making. The thin edge of the spearthrower is rubbed, under considerable pressure, across a split log until the heat from the friction ignites the powdered wood-dust. This smouldering wood-dust, placed in a pad of dry grass and held in the wind or blown upon, soon bursts into flame.

(*iii*) *Wooden Carrying Dish* (*Fig.* 2C)

As the bean-tree, with its soft, easily carved wood, does not grow in the desert country of the Pitjandjara tribe, the carrying dishes of the women have to be cut, with considerable labour, from a hollow bole of one of the large eucalyptus-trees. As the wood is hard and dense, and the only tools available for this heavy cutting are crude, unflaked boulders picked up from the hillside, the manufacture of one of these dishes requires several days of hard continuous labour.[2] The adze stone on the end of the spearthrower, however, is often used to finally smooth the dish.

This dish has many uses:

(*a*) As a baby's cradle.[3]

(*b*) As a food and water container.

(*c*) As a winnowing bowl, which the woman, by a complicated rocking movement, uses to separate the grass seed from the husks and sand.

(*d*) As a mixing dish, where the ground seed is kneaded into cakes preparatory to cooking them in the hot sand and ashes.

(*e*) As a hold-all, in which the woman carries her personal possessions and sometimes her baby, from one camp to the other.

(*iv*) *Wooden Digging Stick* (*Fig.* 2B)

The digging stick of the Pitjandjara women is no more than a mulga stake about four feet long and two inches in diameter, one end of which has been sharpened to a chisel point in the fire. This tool is used for unearthing small creatures, uncovering the roots of trees in the search for wood grubs, or digging out underground tubers.

(*v*) *Grinding Stones* (*Fig.* 2D, E)

The stones used for reducing the grass-seed into flour are particularly simple, the upper mill-stone (Fig. 2D) is a more or less pancake-

[2] Love (1942, pp.215-17) describes the manufacture of one of these wooden dishes with unflaked stone tools.

[3] Mountford (1948, p.171) illustrates one of these wooden carrying dishes being used as a cradle.

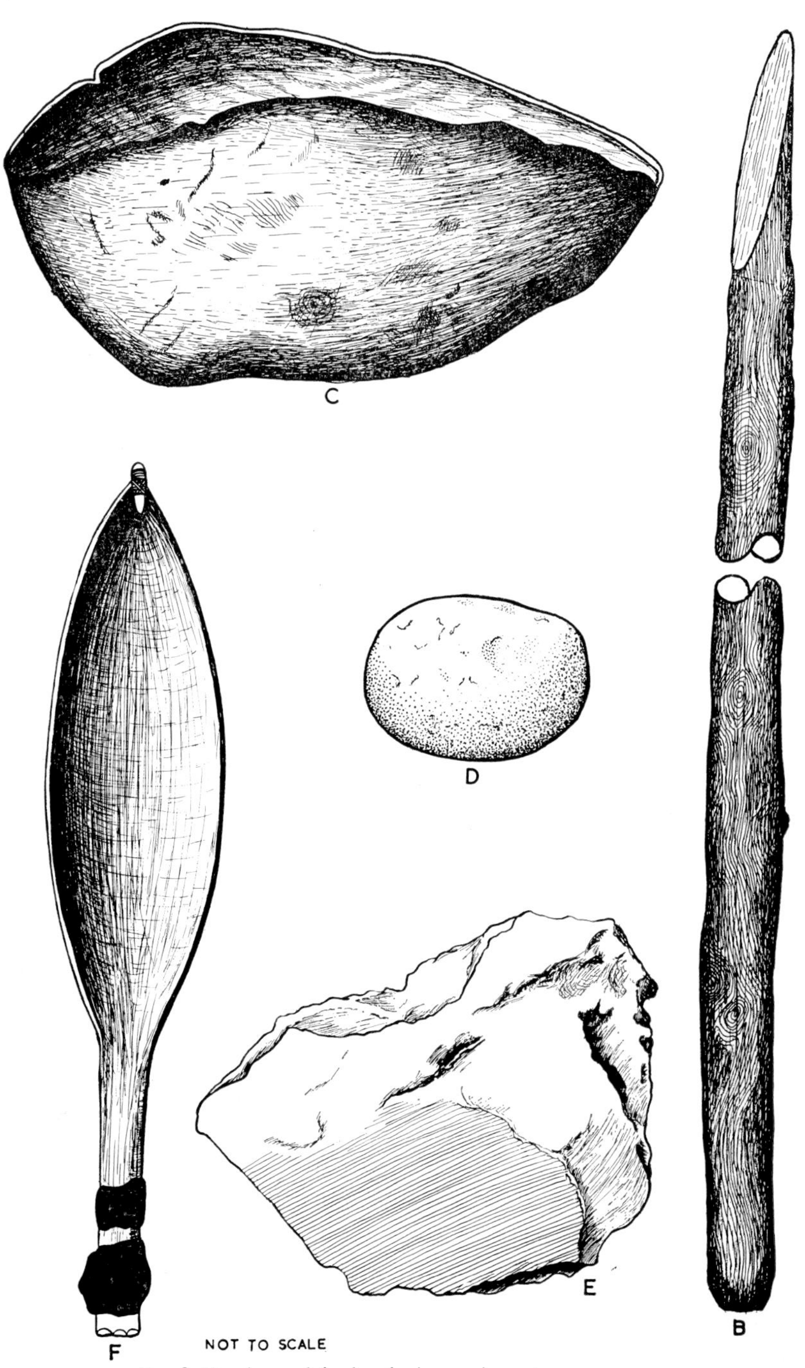

FIG. 2. Hunting and food-gathering equipment.

shaped boulder, two to three inches in diameter, and the lower (Fig. 2E) a simple flat slab of stone, seldom more than six to eight inches across, which appears to be acceptable as long as it has a small flat grinding surface, and is not too heavy to carry. See Pl. 3A.

To show the poverty of the material culture of the men and women of the Pitjandjara tribe it is necessary to compare their equipment with that used by the aborigines who live in more favoured parts of the continent.

The aborigines living on the sea-coast and along the banks of the larger rivers usually have, in addition to their basic food-gathering equipment and weapons of offence, fishing equipment, in the form of nets, fish spears, and other aids for capturing the water creatures. Some tribes also possess watercraft, although the distribution of this form of transport is very uneven in Australia; along vast stretches of the coastline the native population has no means whatever of travelling by water.

Nevertheless, the bulk of the native people use a much lesser number of tools to gain a livelihood. The following list, taken from Spencer and Gillen's *Native Tribes of Central Australia* (1899, pp.567-614), is, with the exception of a few personal ornaments and ceremonial objects, typical of the equipment used over most of inland Australia. The men's hunting equipment includes:

(*i*) *Spears*

These are of four kinds: (*a*) stone-headed spears; (*b*) wooden spears with barbs carved in the shaft; (*c*) heavy unbarbed spears with a lance-shaped point; and (*d*) a light barbed wooden spear similar to that used by the Pitjandjara (Fig. 2A).

(*ii*) *Spearthrowers*

Two kinds of spearthrowers are in common use: (*a*) a somewhat oval, hollow weapon with a cutting edge of stone at one end and a throwing peg at the other (Fig. 2F); and (*b*) a similar weapon on which the cutting stone is replaced by a wooden knob.

(*iii*) *Boomerangs*

These are curved hunting weapons, about thirty inches long, convex on one face and flat on the other.

(*iv*) *Cutting Tools*

Three types of cutting tools are employed: (*a*) a flaked stone mounted on a short stick with a mass of spinifex gum; (*b*) a mounted stone axe, the blade being a pebble of tough stone ground to a sharp edge at one end; and (*c*) stone knives made from a triangular flake of fine quartzite mounted on a short handle with spinifex gum.

The equipment of the women consists of:

(*i*) *Carrying Dishes*

Dishes for permanent use are cut from the soft wood of the bean-tree; others, made in a few minutes from the thick bark of a eucalpyt, are discarded immediately after use.

PLATE 2. Hunting and food-gathering equipment: A, Woman grinding wongona seed (digging stick not shown); B, Man with spear and spearthrower.

(*ii*) *String Carrying Bags*

The string used in the construction of these bags is made by spinning the fibres of certain plants on a primitive spindle. The bags are either carried over the shoulder or by a line across the forehead.

(*iii*) *Digging Stick*

This implement, like that used by the Pitjandjara women (Fig. 2B), is made from a mulga stake and sharpened at one end.

(iv) Grinding Stones

Two types of grinding stones are employed to reduce the grass-seed into a coarse flour; a small flattened pebble for the upper mill-stone (Fig. 2D), and a much larger flat stone for the lower.

In addition to this equipment, Spencer and Gillen list the following offensive and defensive weapons: (*a*) fighting stick; (*b*) fighting pick made of a triangular flake of stone mounted on a wooden handle; (*c*) hooked boomerang; and (*d*) wooden shield.

Chapter 3

MEANS OF GAINING A LIVELIHOOD IN THE DESERT

With only limited equipment to aid the Pitjandjara aborigines in their search for food, the desert is a hard taskmaster, and life within its boundaries strenuous and full of hardship. Long, tiring journeys in the blazing heat of summer or the cold of winter are part of the daily round; food and water are often scarce, and hunger an ever-present hazard. But these hardships are the life pattern of the desert aborigines, patiently and stoically endured. Only a people intensively trained, as are the Pitjandjara, in the lore of the desert and its food resources could live and multiply under such arid conditions, and the gathering of food is the most important part of their lives.

All members of the family group from the small children to the old men and women are engaged in the continuous search for food, each one having a profound knowledge of the rhythm of the country. From earliest childhood they have learnt almost unconsciously the time of the ripening and fruiting of the vegetable foods and where they are most plentiful; the season of the year when the reptiles wake from their winter sleep; when the animals reproduce; and when and where there is water to drink. The aborigines have also developed a calendar based on the movements of the heavenly bodies, the flowering of certain trees and grasses, the mating calls of the local birds, the arrival of the migrants, and many other signs not known to the white man. All these have a relationship to the food cycle on which their lives depend.

Unlike those who live in the more favoured parts of Australia, the desert people cannot make their camp on a sea coast or the banks of some lily-covered lagoon and be assured of an ample supply of food for weeks or months. They can seldom remain in any one place for more than a few days: the women quickly exhaust the supplies of grass-seed, yams and fruit within walking distance of their camp, while the hunting activities of the men and the presence of so many people near the water supply soon drive the animals and larger birds to another locality. The wandering then starts afresh as the family moves to another place in their tribal country, where experience has taught them there will be food and water.

To show the high degree of skill and organization employed to capture the desert creatures, two methods of hunting will be described: the hunting of the euro, a large kangaroo-like creature that lives only in the hills, and the hunting of the red kangaroo whose home is on the open plains.

The euro is a singularly difficult creature to capture in its native habitat. Its rusty-red fur so matches the colour of the rocks that it is not easy to see; its keen hearing quickly detects the approach of danger, and the speed with which it hops from one rocky foothold to the other makes it impossible for either men or dogs to run it down.

Some parts of the southern Musgrave Ranges, where a number of small rocky hills are isolated from each other by open grassy flats, are excellent hunting grounds for euros. These creatures, who shun the open plains where their colour makes them conspicuous, always choose the shortest routes between one hill and the next, routes which, in the course of time, become well-defined paths. By making use of these paths the aborigines have developed a system of hunting perfected by generations of experiment and practice. The method is simple. The huntsmen, concealed behind trees or light brush shelters, are posted along the track chosen for the day's hunt. The remainder of the men, who constitute the beaters, start at the distant end of one hill and move toward the spear-men, lighting the spinifex as they go. The euros travel ahead of the fire until they reach their only way of escape, the path that leads to the distant hill. There is danger behind and apparent safety in front. The native, standing perfectly still with his spear poised ready to throw, waits until the euro is within a few yards before he casts his weapon. It is a lucky beast that escapes, for even if the spear does not kill, it pierces the skin of the creature and so retards its speed of escape that it is easy to capture.

The red kangaroo of the plains is sometimes speared in a somewhat similar manner but the method of driving is different, for the kangaroo fears the hills as much as the euro does the plains. Nevertheless, when these creatures are travelling to a favourite feeding ground, they tend to follow the same path. Several hunters take up their positions on one of these tracks, while others quietly disturb the feeding kangaroos and shepherd them toward the waiting men. The spear-men are able to stand in almost clear view of the oncoming prey to throw their spears, because a kangaroo, when escaping from its enemies, takes little notice of anyone standing without movement alongside the track, its attention being concentrated on the path in front and the danger behind.

The aborigines are also so skilful in the art of stalking that they can walk up to a kangaroo on an open plain and spear it. On first sighting his prey, the hunter, taking advantage of every tree and shrub, creeps towards the unsuspecting kangaroo until nothing but the open plain separates the hunter from his quarry. Knowing that the kangaroo is alarmed only by movement the hunter, waiting until the animal puts its head down to feed, walks boldly but slowly into the open with his spear poised ready for casting. As soon as the creature raises its head to search for danger, the aboriginal stops and remains absolutely still until the kangaroo again puts its head down to feed. Patiently, the hunter moves forward, a few steps at a time, until less than twenty yards separate him from the feeding kangaroo. As in the hunting of the euro, the spear, when cast, seldom kills, but so retards the movement of the creature that the chase is short and the end certain.[1]

Although the men's contribution to the aborigine's larder consists, almost entirely, of the flesh of the larger creatures, the women's contribution is made up of many kinds of food, some of which are listed below:

(*i*) *Cereals*: seeds of various grasses; seeds of munyelroo, a species of portulaca; seeds of the various acacias, particularly those of the mulga (*Acacia aneura*); seeds of the desert kurrajong; underground tubers of many kinds; roots of certain young trees.

(*ii*) *Fruits*: wild peaches (*Eucarva persicarius*); wild oranges (*Caparis mitchelli*); figs (*Ficus platypoda*); black plums (unidentified); galls on mulga-trees; galls on bloodwood-trees.

(*iii*) *Flesh Foods*: lizards; bandicoots; snakes; rabbits and other small creatures; wood-grubs, various; termites.

Although the gathering of the foods by the women requires an intimate knowledge of when and where the fruits and grasses are ready to collect and the time when the smaller creatures are available, the techniques used in collecting these foods are, in general, comparatively simple, consisting of little more than plucking the fruits from the trees, and digging the tubers or creatures from the ground.

However, to gather the grass-seeds; to separate them from the

[1] Finlayson (1938, pp.63-7) gives a particularly vivid description of a Mala (hare-wallaby) hunt.

husks and the rubbish until they are clean; to reduce them to a coarse flour by means of simple grinding stones; and to bake the flour into an edible cake—all this requires the use of a number of skilful and complex techniques. The making of a cake by a Pitjandjara woman from the seed of wongona grass is an excellent example (Pl. 2).

Having located a spot where the wongona grass has shed its seed, the woman rakes both the dust and the seed into small piles, puts them into her wooden dish (Fig. 2c), and empties them on a flat rock or a patch of clean hard ground. When she has collected sufficient for her needs, or has exhausted the supply, the woman fills her dish with the dust and seed and, standing up, allows the mixture to trickle to the ground beneath. The seed falls almost vertically but most of the dust and the lighter material, such as the husks, is blown to one side by the wind. The woman repeats this winnowing until there is little more than grass-seed and sandy material left.

Placing this residue again into her wooden dish, the woman, by means of a complicated rocking action (which few aboriginal men are able to imitate), causes the clean seed to move to the lower end, and the rubbish and earth to the upper end of the dish. The clean seed is poured on a sheet of bark or a patch of hard ground, and the rubbish thrown away. The woman repeats this action several times until the seed is thoroughly clean. The wongona seed, ground into a coarse flour between the grinding stones (illustrated in Pl. 2A) is then mixed with water into a small cake and buried in the hot sand and ashes of the camp fire until cooked.

Although the aboriginal woman may have spent an hour or more collecting, winnowing and grinding the grass-seed, later cooking it in the ashes of the camp fire, the completed cake is seldom larger than a small saucer, a very poor reward for so much effort.

There is a clear-cut division between the food-gathering activities of the men and women. The men, carrying their spears and spearthrower (Pl. 3B), hunt the larger creatures, kangaroos, euros, emus and the larger lizards. The capture of these involves unrestricted movement and often long, tiring journeys. The women, on the other hand, laden with children and their food-gathering equipment, travel by a comparatively direct route from one waterhole to the next, gathering grass-seeds, fruits, small reptiles, wood-grubs and other tit-bits on the way. The aboriginal women are the more reliable of the food-gatherers. Many days the men will return to camp empty-handed, for desert animals are wary and difficult to capture; but the women will always bring in some food, at times not very much nor particularly tasty, but sufficient to keep the family going until the men are more successful in their hunting. Though, in general, the desert does not yield an abundance of food, it is so varied that the aborigines do not suffer from deficiency diseases.

When travelling with the Pitjandjara aborigines it was noticed that, when an aboriginal came into camp with a kangaroo he had speared and probably carried several miles, he threw the carcass down at the feet of another aboriginal, seated himself in the shade of a tree, and apparently took no further interest in the matter. The recipient who cooked the creature kept the dainties such as the liver, the heart and other tit-bits for himself, and portioned out the rest of the meat, even the best joints, to other members of the group, leaving the least desirable parts of the kangaroo, ribs, neck and head, for the hunter.

This food-distribution system, which works so smoothly that its operation is not immediately evident, applies at all times to everyone in the family group, whether the amount of food is large or small, or the participants men or women. In the long run, however, everyone receives an equal share of the food brought in, because the donor of today will be the recipient of tomorrow.

There appears to be, however, a much wiser purpose behind this custom than the mere distribution of food. The government of the tribe is in the hands of the old men; it is they who have the power to make the decisions and to ensure their enforcement. If the skilled hunters, usually young men, were allowed to distribute their own catch, they could, by bartering their game for privileges, so undermine the authority of the old men that the social balance of the tribe would be upset. But, under aboriginal law, the aboriginal hunter, young or old, gains no material advantage from his hunting prowess. His skill is of more value to his people than to him; his pleasure is in the joy of achievement and the approbation of his fellows, powerful factors in any community, primitive or modern.

Chapter 4

THE TRIBAL ORGANIZATION

THE customs that govern the distribution of food are an extension of the web of ancient laws and rituals that bind the men and women of the Pitjandjara tribe so closely together. These bonds are of many forms: a reciprocal system of social relationships, with their attendant privileges, expressed through the cultural outlets of myth, song and ceremony; their common language, and the beliefs in the mythical origin of the natural features of each of the clan territories. Each of these is the home of a self-governing family group, the men believing that they are direct descendants of the mythical creator[1] of the land in which they live. To give a clearer picture of these clan territories, and the relationship that the occupants bear to each other, two belonging to Ayers Rock will be described.

My informant, Balinga, a Mala (hare-wallaby) man is a member of the totemic group whose clan territory is on the northern side of Ayers Rock, while I, who am looked upon by the Ayers Rock aborigines as a Kunia (carpet-snake) man, belong to the clan who live along the southern face. The boundaries of the clan territories at Ayers Rock (Fig. 3), are an excellent example of how accurately they are defined.

The clan lands of the Mala group extend from the camp of the old man guarding the Mala women at Tabudja (A, Fig. 3), along the northern face of the Rock to the southern end of the initiation cave of the Mala on the western face (B, Fig. 3). The Kunia clan territory which joins that of the Mala (A, Fig. 3), extends along the eastern, southern and western sides, where it again joins the boundary of the Mala clan territory (B, Fig. 3).[2]

The inhabitants of a particular clan territory normally gain a livelihood within its boundaries, and seldom leave it except on special occasions, such as the initiation of the youths (which is

[1] These mythical creators will be referred to as the totemic beings.

[2] There are a hundred, and possibly more, of these clan territories within the area of the Pitjandjara tribe. The boundaries of clan territories in the Mann Ranges are as clearly defined as those at Ayers Rock (Mountford, Field Notes, 1940).

largely a tribal matter), or the performance of some important totemic ceremony involving the participation of many people. At times of food and water shortage in a particular territory, however, its members are allowed to camp and hunt in the country of one of its neighbours until the crisis has passed.

The aborigines who live in one of the clan territories at Ayers Rock, for example those of the Mala, are all members of an extended family, each of whom are related to the other by either birth or marriage. The males, i.e. grandfathers, fathers, sons and possibly grandsons, with their children all belong to the same totemic group, that is, the Mala. Their wives, born in some other clan territory, will, of course belong to a different totem.

The Pitjandjara tribe, whose social structure is much simpler than that of the adjoining tribes, is divided into two intermarrying groups, or moieties, i.e. the *Nananduraḳa* (my people), and the *Tanamildjan* (the other folk).[3] The terms are reciprocal; Balinga, my informant, would refer to his own Mala clan group as *Nananduraḳa*, and to mine (the Kunia) as *Tanamildjan*. I, in turn, would call my Kunia relatives *Nananduraḳa* and the Mala people of Balinga's clan *Tanamildjan*.

A man or a woman can only marry a member of the opposite moiety, i.e. *Tanamildjan*. Referring again to the specific situation at Ayers Rock, the men of the Mala totem, being *Tanamildjan* to my totem, would tend to marry, and probably would, in most instances, marry the women of my totem (the Kunia); whilst my relatives, the Kunia men, would tend to marry the women of the Mala totem. However, all children born to men belonging to my clan would be of the Kunia totem, and those born to men belonging to the northern side of Ayers Rock would be Mala people. To the boys, the clan territory of their father is their permanent home. The women, on their marriage, although they still retain their totemic name, will live in the country of their husbands.

The government of the tribe is in the hands of the well-informed old men, not the physically active youth. It is the old men who maintain the ancient laws and decide the correct time for the performance of the rituals on which the social and philosophical life of the tribe depend. The full knowledge of the mythical past and the rites associated with it belongs only to these tribal elders.

It is not, therefore, the duty of a professional or priestly class to preserve the traditional myths and their rites but of a number of groups of initiated men, each of whom is responsible for memoriz-

[3] Both Tindale (1935, pp.20-3) and Elkin (1939, p.213) refer to these moieties as *Nananduraka* or *Nanandaga* and *Tanamildjan*.

ing the traditions and songs of their clan territories and transmitting them unaltered to the succeeding generations. For instance, those aborigines belonging to the Mala (hare-wallaby) or the Kunia (carpet-snake) totems of Ayers Rock are the custodians of the mythical stories, songs and rites of their particular clan territory. This means that the full story of even one totemic being (with the exception of the stationary creators), whose route usually extends over considerable distances, is divided among the local groups through which the totemic hero had passed.

The myths of Ayers Rock, and I feel sure, elsewhere in the Pitjandjara country, are of two types: (*a*) the travelling myths, and (*b*) the stationary myths. With the travelling myths, the incidents that happen in one locality (for example, at Ayers Rock, the hare-wallabies, the lizard men or the snakes) would be only one of a long chain of incidents which, if they could be followed, would extend along a route of many hundreds of miles in length. The myth of Orion and the Pleiades has been traced by the author from eastern Western Australia (Warburton Ranges) to Glen Helen in the western MacDonnell Ranges of central Australia, a distance of over four hundred air miles. This however, was not the complete myth; the myth extended eastward and westward from these localities. More recently, in north-western central Australia, I followed the myth of the snake Yarapi for almost three hundred miles. This, however, was only a part of the totemic route.[4] On the other hand, the actors in the stationary myths at Ayers Rock, i.e. the marsupial moles, Itjari-tjari (Pls 85-9), the man and woman Kadidi (Pls 90-1), and the sleepy-lizard, Meta-lungana (Pls 92-7), appear to have originated, and to have always stayed, at Ayers Rock.

[4] Mountford, Field Notes, 1935, 1960.

Part Two

THE BELIEFS OF THE PITJANDJARA

Chapter 5

THE CREATION BELIEFS[1]

THE mythical stories of the Pitjandjara link them closely to their environment. They do not consider themselves the "Lords of Creation", but part of creation itself. The great creators of the animals, the birds, the plants and the topography of the tribal lands, were also the progenitors of the aborigines who live in that country; the same life essence (*ḳurunba*) left behind by those creators to vitalize all living things also provides the aborigines with vitality. The aborigines believe they are an integral part of the life around them, no greater and no less than any of its component parts.

The men and women of the Pitjandjara trace their very existence back to creation or *tjuḳurapa* times. The central meaning of *tjuḳurapa* is that of a sacred period in the long-distant times when the great totemic heroes performed a succession of mighty deeds. These *tjuḳurapa* heroes made the lands of the Pitjandjara; the food creatures that live thereon; the first spears and spearthrowers for the men to capture the desert animals; and the wooden dish and the digging stick to assist the women in their everlasting search for food.

The same creators also decreed the laws that govern all aspects of the daily and sacred life; the relationship of each member of the tribe to the other; the ceremonies to be performed before men can be admitted more deeply into the secret life; and the supernatural penalties that all will suffer if they disobey the laws of those ancient times. These stories, or myths of *tjuḳurapa* times are accepted by the aborigines as a record of absolute truth and an answer to all the questions in the daily life of the people. It is by the continuous re-enactment of these myths by ceremony, song and mime that the accounts of the creation of the world, the exploits of the *tjuḳurapa* heroes, and the decrees they promulgated, are kept alive and unaltered in the minds of the Pitjandjara tribesmen. The aboriginal saying, "As it was done in *tjuḳurapa* times, so

[3] Stanner (1956), in his excellent article "The Dreaming", deals fully with this subject.

must it be done today", dominates all aspects of aboriginal thought and behaviour.[2]

An examination of the past of the aborigines suggests the reason for this opposition to change. The aborigines have lived in this country for an unknown, but undoubtedly lengthy, period. The time element matters less than the fact that during that period the aborigines have been almost completely isolated from external influence. To this fact can be added two others; their physical environment, which, within their lifetime has, for all practical purposes, remained unchanged, and the simple unprogressive nature of their tools and weapons.

When we consider these facts—the long period spent in complete isolation in a constant physical environment and with an unprogressive material culture—it becomes clear why sameness, lack of change, fixed routine and regularity are so important in the life of the desert aborigines. We begin to understand the necessity which they attach to keeping life on a routine that is known and can be trusted; lack of change means certainty of expectation. The desert people believe that the pattern of life has always been, and will always remain, the same from the dim times of the remote past to the present and on to the distant future. It is evident, then, that the aborigines would have no history in our sense of the word, no succession of events, no stories of conquests or invasions by conquering people, no records of outstanding personalities or famous men of war.

The aborigines are not interested, as we are, in the episodes of the past. The important things to them are the cycles of life: the development of the individual from infancy to old age; the path of the initiates from ignorance to knowledge; the yearly round of the seasons; the movements of the celestial bodies; and the breeding times of the creatures. These cycles are full of meaning to the native people, but to them the remote past, the present, and the future are and will be changeless.

The Universe of the Pitjandjara

The Pitjandjara believe that their world is flat, and so limited in area that if they travelled to the horizon, which to them is the edge of the universe, they would be in danger of falling into limitless space. The Pitjandjara universe has two levels, the earth, *puna*, the home of the aboriginal men and women, and the celestial world, *ilkari*, in which reside the people of the sky, many of whom once

[2] Undoubtedly, small changes are continuously taking place, but, in general, these changes are not conscious, but caused either by faulty memories or wrong interpretations of the ancient beliefs.

lived on earth during *tjukurapa* times.[3] In this sky world, there is an abundance of food, shelter and water.[4]

In the beginning, that is, before there was any life in the universe, the world was a flat featureless plain extending to the horizon, unbroken by a mountain range, watercourse, or any major topographical feature. Then, at some period in the long-distant past known to the Pitjandjara as *tjukurapa* times, giant semi-human beings, resembling one or another of the creatures in appearance, but behaving like human beings, rose out of the featureless plain where for countless ages they had been slumbering, and started to wander in criss-cross routes over the countryside. And, as they wandered, these mythical people behaved in the same manner as the aborigines of today: made fire, dug for water, performed ceremonies, fought each other, and so on. During the whole of this period, the earth remained flat and more or less featureless.[5] When, mysteriously, *tjukurapa* times came to an end, at every place where one or another of the heroes had performed any task, a mountain range, an isolated hill, a valley, a watercourse, or some other natural feature was created. The bodies, too, of the *tjukurapa* men and women were often transformed into isolated boulders or piles of rocks.[6]

When the aborigines were asked what brought about this remarkable change, they said they did not know, but felt sure that some wise old men of an earlier generation could have told me. Since these old men had not passed their knowledge on to the succeeding generations, there was no one today who could answer my question.

These great creators of the aborigines' land, were, at the same time, the forbears of the tribe; so that there are aborigines of the carpet-snake, hare-wallaby, sleepy-lizard, marsupial mole, willy-wagtail totems, and so on, all of whom believe that they are the direct descendants of one or another of the *tjukurapa* heroes of the long-distant past. Since everyone claims descent from these mythical

[3] There is no evidence of a Pitjandjara belief in an underground world, such as the home of the *iruntarinia* recorded by Spencer and Gillen (1899, p.424). The Tiwi of Melville Island, on the other hand, believe that their universe has four levels, a subterranean world, *ilara*; the world on which the aborigines live; the world of the star people, *juwuka*; and an upper world, *tuniruna*, the dry weather home of the thunderstorms, lightning and monsoon rains. (Mountford, 1958, p.170.)

[4] The Pitjandjara do not appear to have any conception of a future life. (Mountford, 1948, p.113.)

[5] During a recent address, T. G. H. Strehlow mentioned that, according to the Aranda beliefs, the natural features were created by the mythical people at the same time as they moved across the countryside. The Pitjandjara, on the other hand, claimed that there was no change in the topography until the close of the creation period.

[6] The aborigines believe that these transformed bodies, often small isolated boulders, are a concentrated life essence, *kurunba* or *kuranita*, of that particular totemic being. The carpet-snake stones at Kuniapiti, at Ayers Rock (Pls 29B, 30B), or that of the sleepy-lizard (Pl. 96B), are typical examples. If the aborigines rub one or another of those stones (there are many in the Pitjandjara country), at the same time chanting the correct song, the life essence, *kurunba*, contained within the stone will rise in the air "like a mist" (an aboriginal explanation), and, by impregnating the female of that particular species, increase the food supplies.

beings, and each, in turn, lives in the land created by his immediate progenitor, it follows that every man, woman and child is linked, both by myth and genealogy, with his tribal country. The following study of the topographical features of Ayers Rock and the myths that explain their origin is an excellent example of the intimate links that exist between the aborigines and their land.

[7] Harney (1960) pp. 63-76 in his paper "Ritual and Behaviour at Ayers Rock", also deals with the mythology of Ayers Rock. As the majority of Mr Harney's statements do not agree with my research, I will not refer to them in the later descriptions.

Chapter 6

THE TOPOGRAPHY OF AYERS ROCK

Ayers Rock (Pls 3-4 and Fig. 3), a huge monolith about two hundred miles south-east of Alice Springs, is an important place in the lives of the aborigines of the Pitjandjara tribe. There are eleven waterholes at Ayers Rock, some permanent, some semi-permanent. Mutitjilda, on the south side, is one of the most reliable waterholes in the Pitjandjara country, and it would be seldom, if ever, that one could not get water at Kandju soak, on the western side, by digging in the sand near by. The numerous caves around the base of the Rock provide warm, roomy shelters for the aborigines, while, before the arrival of the white man, the euros, bandicoots, wallabies and other small creatures living among the boulders at the base of the Rock, and the kangaroos, emus and dingoes visiting the waterholes to drink, would have provided the aborigines with ample flesh food.

Also, since Ayers Rock is a huge boulder, without any covering of earth, all the rain that falls on its surface is shed on the plain below. This run-off has created a narrow fertile band at the base of the Rock, on which there are in their season abundant fruits, tubers and grass-seeds. It is likely that the aborigines at Ayers Rock were living under better conditions of food, shelter and water than any other totemic group in the Pitjandjara country. The fact that there was sufficient food and water at Ayers Rock to allow the large number of aborigines necessary to carry out the elaborate rituals of initiation, to stay long enough to complete the task would give Ayers Rock an even greater importance in the minds of the Pitjandjara tribesmen.[1]

Ollier and Tuddenham (1962, pp.257-76), in their study of the geomorphology of the area, give a general account of three inselbergs: Mt Conner, a flat-topped mesa; Ayers Rock, fifty miles farther west, a huge dome-shaped monolith; and twenty miles still farther west, a group of high domes, known by the aboriginal name of Katatjuta, of which Mt Olga is the highest point.

[1] Initiation ceremonies of the desert people often have to be curtailed because there is insufficient food and water in the locality to support so many people for any length of time.

PLATE 3. A, Ayers Rock from the west; B, Ayers Rock from the south.

Plate 4. A, Ayers Rock from the east; B, Ayers Rock from the north.

According to these writers (1962, p.262), "Ayers Rock is a huge monolith rising to the height of two thousand, eight hundred and twenty feet above sea-level, and eleven hundred and forty feet above the plain, with a perimeter of approximately five and a half miles. In plan, Ayers Rock is roughly kite-shaped [Fig. 3], and in section, a rough domed shape with a flattened top, but this shape depends on the direction from which it is viewed [Pls 3, 4]. The unity and isolation of the monolith is truly remarkable, but the lack of perspective on the plains country prevents appreciation of its true size. . . .

"Ayers Rock consists of a coarse arkose grit, with rare bands of conglomerate containing pebbles up to an inch in diameter. The beds dip approximately south-west at an angle of eighty degrees but the Rock is exceedingly massive and bedding can be seen better at a distance than close-up. . . . There is no doubt . . . that the grooves, seen on the top of the Rock are along the lines of bedding. [Fig. 3.]

"The sides of Ayers Rock are very steep (up to eighty degrees), and in most parts of the perimeter they have become concave toward ground level, and, in a few places, this concavity has developed to such an extent that an overhang is found. . . . The top surface . . . consists of a series of closely spaced ridges and furrows with a relief of 6 to 15 feet. These [furrows] carry over to the sides where the largest run-offs have formed waterfalls, some up to three hundred feet in height. The waterfalls are marked by a dark stain of uncertain origin. Small caves and pockets are also formed in many parts of the Rock."

Ollier and Tuddenham also point out that the Rock, owing to the spalling of small flakes from its surface, is continually sloughing off skins of equal thickness. This form of weathering, at approximately the same rate at all parts of the Rock, is gradually decreasing its size without appreciably altering its original form.

The aborigines' conception of the Rock is a complete antithesis to this viewpoint. To them, Ayers Rock, their Uluru, has remained unchanged and unchanging from when, at the close of the creation period, it rose miraculously out of a large flat sandhill. The aborigines believe that ten different totemic mythical beings created the topography of Ayers Rock. The major mythological details are shown on the map in Fig. 3, and the minor ones in Pls 3-104.

Chapter 7

THE MYTHS OF AYERS ROCK

MOST of the southern face of Ayers Rock was created by the battle between the Liru (poisonous snakes) and the Kunia (carpet-snakes). Two other totemic creatures also created minor portions of the southern face: Linga (sand-lizard), and Metalungana (sleepy-lizard). The activities of the Mala (hare-wallaby) people were responsible for most of the northern face and the north-westerly corner of Ayers Rock, although, here again, other totemic creatures created some part of the topography, i.e. Linga (sand-lizard); Tjinderi-tjinderiba (willy-wagtail woman) and her children, the Yulanya; Kulpunya, the spirit dingo, who destroyed most of the Mala men and their families; and Lunba, the kingfisher woman, who tried to protect them.

Three other minor totemic beings are associated with the western face, Kandju (sand-lizard), the creator of the Kandju soak and the surrounding topography; Itjari-tjari (marsupial mole), who created a number of caves and potholes on the surface of the western side; and the man and woman, Kadidi, whose camps were transformed into a pile of boulders on the south-western corner. The exploits of these many totemic beings, and the natural features created by their exploits, will now be described in detail.

(*a*) *The Carpet-snakes, Kunia, and the Venomous Snakes, Liru*

The aborigines believe that during the *tjukurapa* (creation) times, a large number of non-venomous snakes, the Woma (*Aspidites ramsayi*) and the Kunia (carpet-snakes, *Liasis childreni*), lived at an unlocalized place called Pugabuga,[1] some distance east of Mt Conner.

After a while the snake people, becoming dissatisfied with the surroundings of Pugabuga, decided to leave and travel westward. But when they reached Maratjara, a spring near the deserted Lyndavale station, the snakes split into two parties. The Woma, who now

[1] Pugabuga would, almost certainly, be some form of water supply, most likely a spring or rockhole; mythical snakes, particularly the non-venomous species, are almost always associated with water.

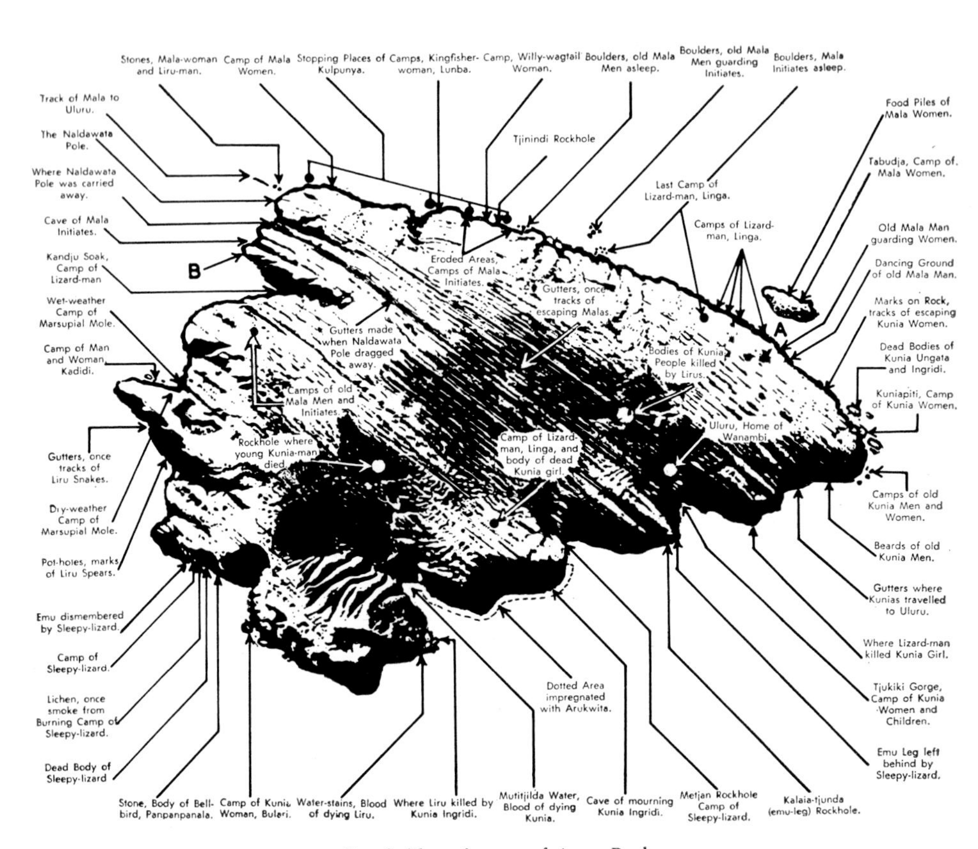

FIG. 3. Totemic map of Ayers Rock.

live exclusively in the sandhill country, remained near Maratjara, while the Kunia continued their journey until they came to a large flat sandhill in the middle of which Uluru water was situated.[2] A number of the Kunia camped at Uluru water, while others, mostly old people, women and children stayed either at the south-easterly corner, or in Tjukiki gorge, on the south side (Pls 5-10 and Fig. 3).

At the close of the creation period, these Kunia people were transformed into natural features. Large boulders in Tjukiki gorge (Pls 6A, 10B) were once the Kunia women seated in their camps; a tall conical slab of rock at the head of the gorge (Pl. 10A) was their wooden carrying dish; the rockhole, Kapi Tjukiki (Fig. 3), their camp fire, and the low bushes on the floor of the gorge, their pubic hairs. The larger boulders on the slopes of the south-eastern corner of Ayers Rock (Pl. 8B) were the Kunia women, and the smaller, their children. The camps of the women are now large caves above the aboriginal standing on the boulder, and those of the children, small caves such as those on the lower right of the illustration.

On the plain beneath, the long boulder in Pl. 8A was a Kunia woman, and the smaller her children; that in Pl. 6B, an old woman asleep, and in Pls 5B and 7B old Kunia men, lying asleep in the sun. The deep ridges on the side of the Rock (Pl. 7A) were once the tracks made in the sand by the mythical carpet-snake people as they travelled to and from the Uluru waterhole; the gutters in Plate 5A the beards of the old men; and the caves in the face of the cliff (Pl. 9A) places where one or another of the Kunia people had once camped. Smaller circular depressions on the summit of the Rock (Pl. 9B) were made when one or another of the carpet-snake people rested during *tjukurapa* times in the soft sand of Uluru. During that period everything went well at Uluru, the women setting out every day to gather the vegetable foods, the yams, the grass-seeds and the fruits, and the men capturing the kangaroos, the emus, the wallabies and other creatures.

At the same time as the carpet-snake people had settled at Uluru, a party of young and old venomous snake-men, the Liru, under the leadership of Kulikudjeri, were travelling from place to place in the Pitjandjara country, causing a great deal of trouble to the other mythical people.

Coming from the west, the Liru made their camp on the southern end of Katatjuta.[3] The huge dome (Pl. 11B) adjacent to Mt Olga,

[2] As mentioned earlier, this sandhill, at the close of the creation period, became the present-day Ayers Rock (Fig. 3).

[3] I have called the whole assemblage of these immense domes by the apt aboriginal name of Katatjuta (*Kata*—heads; *tjuta*—many) reserving Giles's original name, Mt Olga, for the highest point.

PLATE 5. The carpet-snakes, Kunia: A, Gutters once beard of old Kunia man, eastern Ayers Rock; B, Boulders, once Kunia men asleep.

TOTEMIC CREATURES OF AYERS ROCK

A. The Venomous Snake, Liru. B. The Carpet Snake, Kunia. C. The Hare Wallaby, Mala. D. The Spirit Dingo, Kulpunya. E. The Kingfisher Woman, Lunba. F. The Sleepy Lizard, Meta-lungana. G. The Sand Lizard, Linga. H. The Marsupial Mole, Itjari-tjari. J. The Willy-wagtail, Tjinderi-tjinderiba.

PLATE 6. The carpet-snakes, Kunia: A, Tjukiki Gorge, camp of Kunia women; B, Old Kunia woman asleep.

PLATE 7. The carpet-snakes, Kunia: A, Vertical gutters formed when Kunia travelled to Uluru; B, Boulder, once Kunia man asleep.

PLATE 8. The carpet-snakes, Kunia: A, Boulders, once Kunia women and children; B, Kunia women and children near their camps.

PLATE 9. The carpet-snakes, Kunia: A, Caves, once camps of Kunia men and women; B, Places on summit of rock where Kunia people rested.

PLATE 10. The carpet-snakes, Kunia: A, Long boulder, once wooden dish of Kunia women at Tjukiki Gorge; B, Boulders, once Kunia women and children at Tjukiki Gorge.

the highest point of Katatjuta, was the camp of the old Liru snakes, and a group of lower domes to the east (Pl. 12A), those of the young snakes. My informant explained that the black water stains and vertical lines of red and green lichen on the fifteen-hundred-foot precipice (Pl. 11B) are the transformed body decorations of the old Liru men. After a while, the younger snake-men, anxious to cause more trouble, left their camp at Katatjuta (Pl. 12A) and travelled to Uluru to attack and destroy the harmless carpet-snakes, leaving the older Liru men behind in their camp at Katatjuta (Pl. 11B).

The young Liru, carrying spears, spearthrowers, stone knives and wooden clubs, approached Uluru from the south-west, the many desert oaks on the sandhills (Pl. 11A) being the metamorphosed bodies of the invading enemy. The Liru men assembled on two stony pavements (Pl. 12B) about four hundred yards west of Uluru, those on the nearest pavement (Pl. 12B) attacking the carpet-snake people camping at the Uluru water (Fig. 3). The tracks of the Liru men were later transformed into deep gutters on the south-western face of Uluru (Pl. 13A).

The other group of Liru men, who set out from the distant pavement (Pl. 12B), threw a shower of spears at the Kunia men and women living on the southern side of Uluru, who quickly retreated to the eastward. The places where the spears fell in the soft sand were, at the close of the creation period, transformed into numerous potholes in the face of a vertical cliff and the rocks at its base (Pl. 14A, B).

A large split boulder (Pl. 15A) on the south-east of Pl. 14A, B was, in *tjukurapa* times, the body of a Kunia woman, Minma Bulari (*minma*—married woman), who gave birth to a child at this place. The boulder has been hollowed out by differential weathering into a small cave, about nine feet in diameter. Within this cave is another cavity (Pl. 16A), with a small entrance to the larger cave. This cavity was once the womb of Bulari, and the opening to it, the vagina and vulva, out of which her child was born. The lighter marks at the opening and on the pavement at the bottom of the photograph were once the knee-marks of the women who assisted in the confinement. The newly born infant is now an irregularly shaped rock near the mouth of the cave (Pl. 16B) and Bulari's wooden carrying dish, a somewhat hollowed boulder near by (Pl. 15B). According to my informants, the body of Bulari contracted so quickly after the birth of her child that she split open, in the same manner, the aborigines explained, as mud when it dries in a waterhole (Pl. 15A).

PLATE 11. The poisonous snakes, Liru: A, Desert Oaks, once Liru men, advancing on Kunia at Ayers Rock; B, Camp of old Liru men at Katatjuta.

PLATE 12. The poisonous snakes, Liru: A, Camps of young Liru men at Katatjuta; B, Pavements where Liru men assembled at Ayers Rock to attack Kunia.

PLATE 13. The poisonous snakes, Liru: A, Gutters in cliff where once Liru travelled to attack carpet-snakes at Uluru Rockhole; B, Crack in rocks, once knife with which Liru killed young carpet-snake.

Plate 14. The poisonous snakes, Liru: A, Holes in southern face of Ayers Rock where Liru threw spears at carpet-snake people; B, Close-up of holes made by Liru spears.

Plate 15. The carpet-snake woman, Bulari: A, Totemic place of Kunia woman, Bulari; B, Boulder, once wooden carrying dish of Bulari.

PLATE 16. The carpet-snake woman, Bulari: A, Bulari's vagina as she gave birth to child; B, Child born to Bulari.

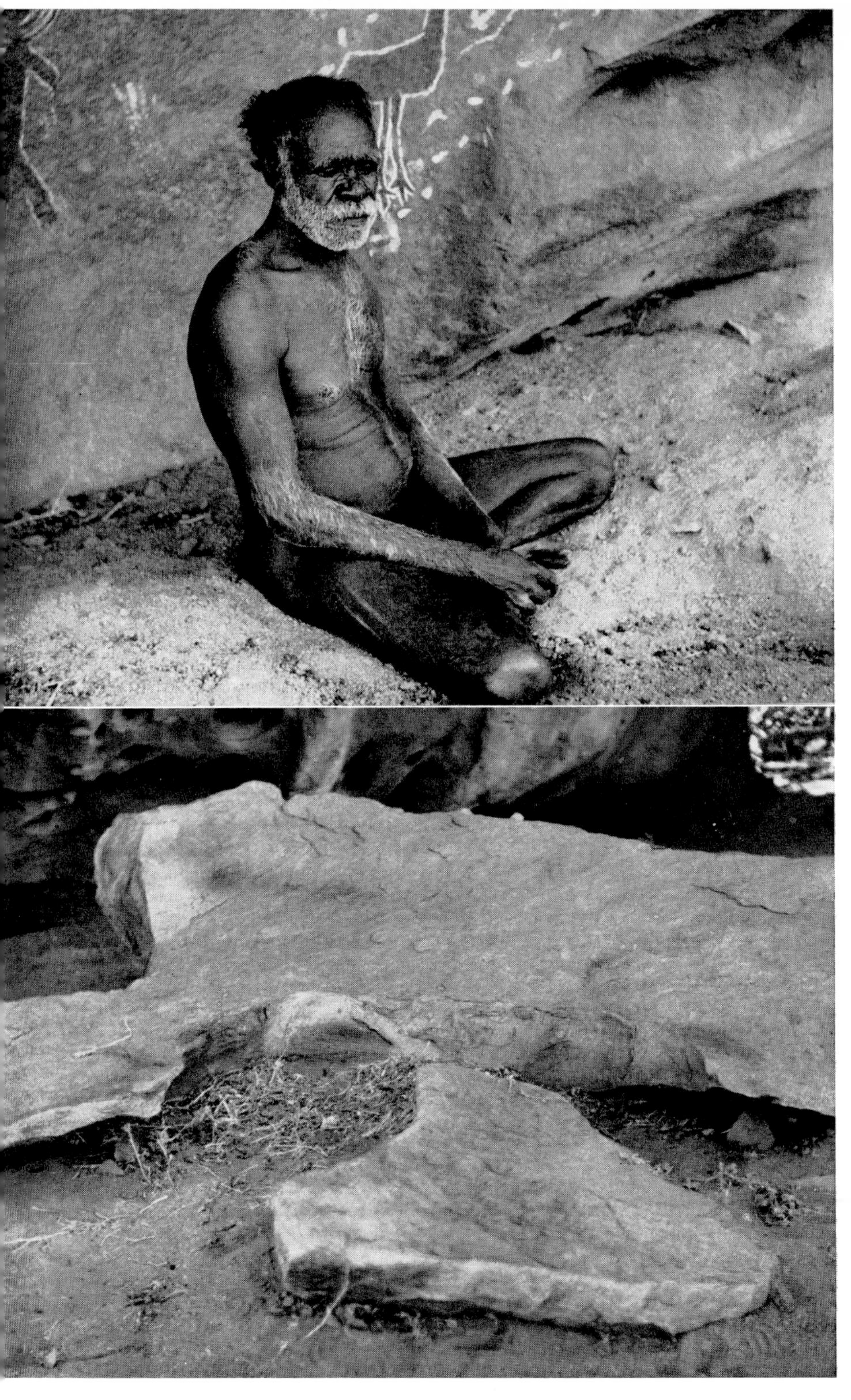

PLATE 17. The carpet-snake woman, Bulari: A. Cave at totemic place where pregnant aboriginal women expect to have easier births; B, Bulari (upper) with newly-born child (lower).

PLATE 18. The carpet-snakes, Kunia: A, Mutitjilda gorge, scene of fight between poisonous and non-poisonous snakes; B, Shield of Kunia man pierced by spear thrown by Liru.

PLATE 19. The carpet-snakes, Kunia: A, Valley in Mutitjilda gorge where young Kunia man died; B, Mutitjilda waterhole.

A few yards to the east of the Bulari stone is a shallow cave in which there are a number of aboriginal paintings. The two irregularly shaped stones in the front of this cave were once Bulari sitting on the ground with the infant resting between her knees (Pl. 17B). The pregnant aboriginal women of today, believing that the spirit of the mythical carpet-snake woman, Bulari, will assist them in having an easier delivery, endeavour to reach this cave to give birth to their infants. The aboriginal in Pl. 17A, a man of the carpet-snake totem, was born in this cave.

When the Liru snake-men approached Bulari's camp, she, taking the newly born child in her arms, advanced toward them spitting out large quantities of *arukwita*, the spirit of disease and death.[4] But, although the *arukwita* killed many of the Liru men, the remainder still advanced, shouting threats and insults at both Bulari and the other carpet-snake men and women. Finding her efforts of little avail, Bulari retreated toward the Mutitjilda gorge (Fig. 3). The mouths of the shouting Liru men are now caves on the surface of a high cliff on the southern side of Uluru (Pl. 21B) and the body of Kulikudjeri, their leader, a large square boulder behind the camp of Bulari.

At Mutitjilda gorge, the Liru leader, Kulikudjeri and a young Kunia man, the son of the Kunia woman, Ingridi, engaged in single combat by standing face to face and gashing each other across the legs with their stone knives.[5] On the western face of Mutitjilda gorge, which is the transformed body of the Liru leader, Kulikudjeri, there are now two long vertical fissures (Pl. 18A). According to my informant, these were once the cuts made in the leg of Kulikudjeri by the stone knife of the young Kunia man, the long cut on the left having been made when the knife was sharp, and the shorter cut after the point had broken.

Kulikudjeri, in spite of his wounds, continued the fight until he succeeded in gashing the leg of his opponent so badly that the young Kunia man started to bleed to death.[6] In his agony the wounded carpet-snake man, bleeding freely, crawled first toward the east then, returning, made his way to what is now the Mutitjilda water, where he rested for a while. Later, delirious from pain and loss of blood, he crawled to the right, making a track which is now

[4] See p.54 for more detailed description. Spencer and Gillen (1899, p.548), describe a magical evil influence, called *arungquiltha* (obviously the same as the Pitjandjara's *arukwita*), which is magically applied, either direct to the victim or to the object used to cause his death, i.e. the pointing bone.

[5] Kulikudjeri's knife is now a large crack in a cliff near the south-western corner of Uluru (Pl. 13B), and a Kunia shield, pierced by a spear thrown by a Liru man, a large oval stone with a hole in the middle on the western side of Mutitjilda gorge (Pl. 18B).

[6] A dark stain, once the blood of the wounded Kunia man (Pl. 24B), extends from the cave of the woman, Kunia Ingridi (Pl. 23A) along the eastern wall of the Mutitjilda gorge to the Mutitjilda waterhole at the head of the gorge (see Fig. 3).

PLATE 20. The poisonous snakes, Liru. A, Holes in cliff, once eyes and nostrils of injured Liru; B, Water-stains, once blood of injured Liru.

PLATE 21. The poisonous snakes, Liru: A, Detached boulder, once nose of injured Liru; B, Holes in cliffs, mouths of shouting Liru.

(Photographs by K. Jose)

PLATE 22. The carpet-snakes, Kunia: A, B, Rockholes above Mutitjilda water where young Kunia man bled to death.

the watercourse that flows into Mutitjilda water (Pl. 19A and Fig. 3). Here the young Kunia man died and the places where he bled to death are now three rockholes, high up the side of the Rock (Pl. 22A, B). The aborigines look on the water in these rockholes, and that in Mutitjilda below (Pl. 19B), as the transformed blood of the dying Kunia man. The aborigines believe that, when the water is getting low in Mutitjilda, they can, by standing at the head of the gorge and shouting "Kuka-kuka" in a loud voice, entice the spirit of the dead Kunia man, who is resident in the upper rockhole (Pl. 22A, B), to send a stream of water to the Mutitjilda waterhole beneath (Pl. 19B).[7]

When Kunia Ingridi, the mother of the young Kunia man, heard that her son had been killed, she became violently angry and, taking her digging stick (first spitting *arukwita* over the weapon to make it more effective) struck the Liru man, Kulikudjeri, such a heavy blow that she cut his nose from his body. This nose is now a huge slab of rock, over seventy feet in height, that has split off the main mass of Uluru (Pls 18A, 21A). The aborigines pointed out four holes, high up the face of the Rock (Pl. 20A), which were once the eyes and nasal passages of Kulikudjeri. The blow from the digging stick and the severing of his nose caused Kulikudjeri to die in great agony. A cliff, immediately under the severed nose (Pl. 20B), is now streaked with water-stains, the transformed blood that once poured from the head of the dying Liru.

After killing her son's adversary, Kunia Ingridi, covering her body with red ochre (a sign of mourning), mourned heartbrokenly over her loss. Part of the eastern wall of the Mutitjilda gorge (which the aborigines look on as the body of Kunia Ingridi) is covered with a red stain (Pl. 23B), and her wide-open mouth, as she gave expression to her grief, a large oval cave (Pl. 23A), caused by differential rock weathering. This cave is east of the entrance to Mutitjilda gorge (Fig. 3).

At the same time as Kunia Ingridi mourned for her lost son, she spat out large quantities of *arukwita* toward her enemies, hoping thereby to kill them all. The white marks at the back of Kunia Ingridi's cave (Pl. 23A), and those mixed with the blood of the dying Kunia man on the walls of the Mutitjilda gorge (Pl. 24B), are all masses of *arukwita*. In fact, Balinga assured me that the area extending from Mutitjilda waterhole, along the base of the Rock to the cave of Kunia Ingridi (Pl. 23A and Fig. 3) is so impregnated with this essence of evil and disease that, if any aboriginal

[7] Several reliable white men have told me that, even in the dry season, water will unexpectedly flow from the upper to the lower waterholes.

PLATE 23. The carpet-snakes, Kunia: A, Cave, mouth of mourning Kunia woman, Ingridi; B, Colour on cliff, once red ochre on Ingridi's body.

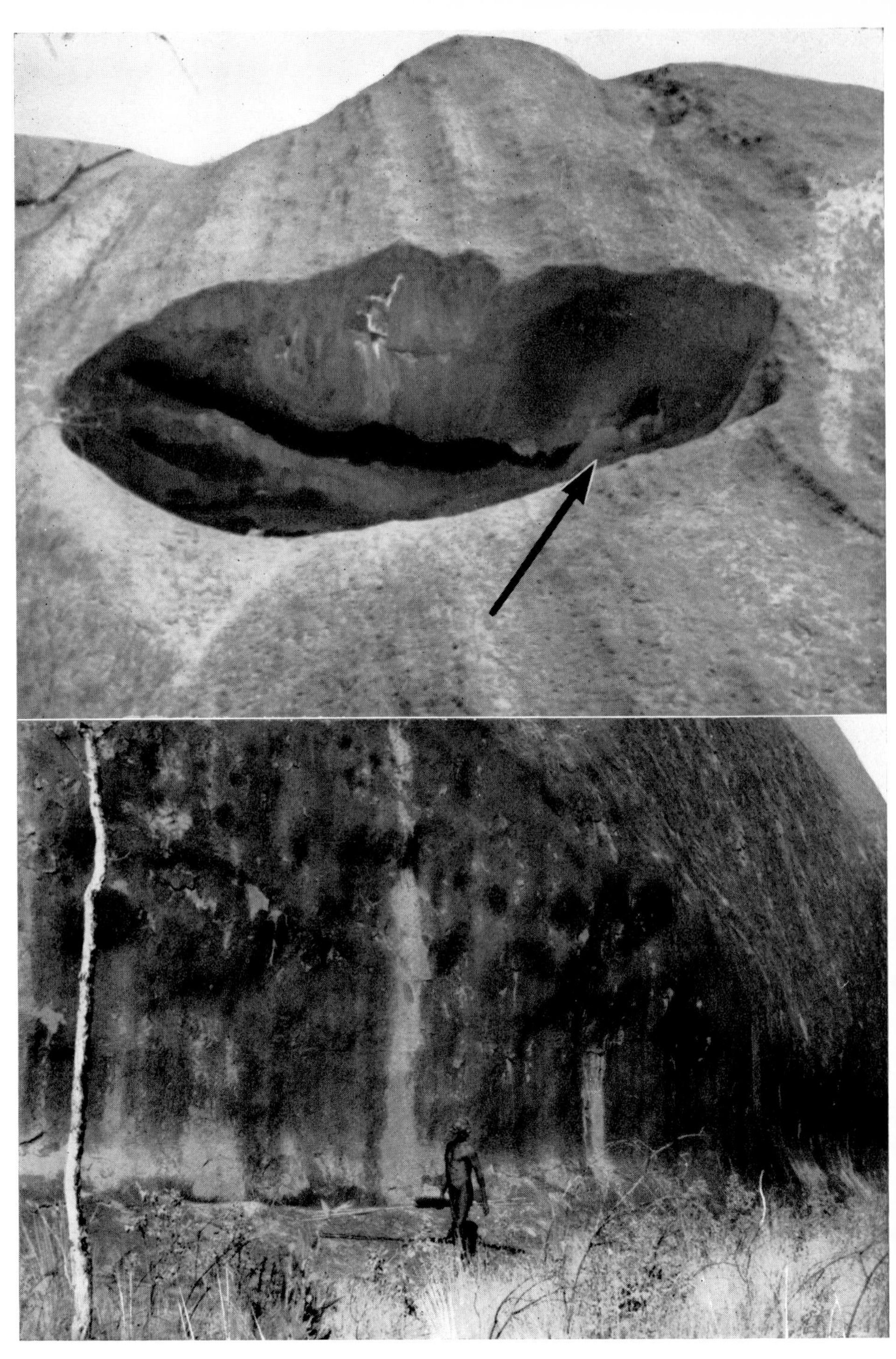

Plate 24. The carpet-snakes, Kunia: A, Arrow indicates the two boulders in cave impregnated with *arukwita*; B, Dark stains on cliff, blood of young dying Kunia.

PLATE 25. The carpet-snakes, Kunia: A, Boulders, body of dead Kunia man on summit, rocks on left, his spears; B, Body of another dead Kunia man on summit.

PLATE 26. The carpet-snakes, Kunia: A, Rocks, upper right, once spear-thrower of dead Kunia; B, Bodies of dead Kunia woman and child.

PLATE 27. The carpet-snakes, Kunia: A, Cleft in rock, once track of Kunia Ingridi; B, Bodies of dead Kunia women, eastern end.

ventures closer than about two hundred yards he will surely die.[8]

There is a song, belonging to the cave of Kunia Ingridi and its *arukwita*, which, when chanted over a pointing bone[9] or any other object, will, if the correct rituals are carried out, so impregnate the object with the spirit of disease and death that it will kill any person toward whom it is pointed. It is also possible for a man to kill himself by the use of the *arukwita* song. This is illustrated by an incident in the Kunia myth.

When an old Kunia man, who was mother's brother to the young Kunia man who had been killed, heard of his death he became so distressed that he took his life by swallowing two small pebbles he had chanted full of *arukwita*. These pebbles are now small spherical boulders on the right-hand side of a cave on the southern side of Uluru (Pl. 24A). My informant, Balinga, told me that when his father heard that the policeman, McKinnon, had shot his son he killed himself by "singing" a piece of kangaroo meat full of *arukwita*, and swallowing it.

At the same time as the fight was taking place between the Liru and Kunia men in Mutitjilda gorge, the other group of Liru men had surrounded and attacked the Kunia people who lived at the Uluru waterhole now on the top of the Rock. Although many were killed, the Kunia woman Ingridi, her husband Kunia Ungata, and a number of carpet-snake women and their children, escaped and fled from Uluru water to Kuniapiti (Pl. 29A), their camp on the eastern end of Ayers Rock. The tracks made by the escaping people are now the horizontal marks of the rock strata on the northern side of Ayers Rock (Pls 27A, 28A).

Many of the long cylindrical boulders on the summit of Ayers Rock lying adjacent to the Uluru rockhole (Fig. 3) are transformed bodies of the dead Kunia people. The long column of rock (Pl. 25A), was once a Kunia man with his spears and spearthrower lying beside him, the group of small cylindrical stones on the left being his transformed spears, and a similar block of stone on the edge of the shadow (Pl. 26A), his spearthrower. Another boulder (Pl. 26B) is the transformed body of a woman and child, and another (Pl. 25B) that of a young Kunia man.

Kuniapiti, the camp of the Kunia people who had fled from their enemies, is shown in Pl. 29A. The large oval-shaped cliff at the back of Kuniapiti was once their windbreak of boughs; the vertical

[8] The aborigines, who contended that the *arukwita* at this place was strong enough to kill even a white man, were surprised that I suffered no harm when, in 1940, I pitched my tent within a few feet of a wall which, they believe, is still impregnated with the spirit of *arukwita*.

[9] Spencer and Gillen (1899, p. 548) describe one of the rituals necessary to impregnate a magical object with the Aranda *arungquiltha*.

PLATE 28. The carpet-snakes, Kunia: A, Strata marks on side of Ayers Rock, once tracks of fleeing carpet-snakes; B, Vertical rock, once digging stick of Kunia Ingridi.

lines, the digging sticks of the women leaning against the windbreak; and the black line leading from the windbreak to the summit, a stream of urine from one of the Kunia women. All the people in this camp, with the exception of Kunia Ungata (Kunia Ingridi's husband) were either women, children or uncircumcised youths, the remainder having been killed by the poisonous snakes, either at the Uluru waterhole or in the Mutitjilda gorge.

When Kunia Ingridi heard of the death of so many of her relatives, she chanted the *arukwita* song to kill herself, her husband and the rest of the carpet-snake people at Kuniapiti. The bodies of these Kunia people were all changed into large and small boulders (Pls 27B, 29A), and their hair into the fig-trees that grow between them. On the lower right of Pl. 29A the long tor-like boulder was once the windbreak of the camp of Kunia Ingridi and her husband. On the eastern side, at ground level, are two cylindrical boulders, the one to the north being the transformed body of the man, Kunia Ungata, (Pl. 29B), and the one to the south (Pl. 30B), that of the woman Kunia Ingridi. These stones are now used for the increase rituals of carpet-snakes. According to some informants, if the aborigines rub one or another of these Kunia stones in the proper season, at the same time chanting the correct song, the life essence, or *kurunba*, of the carpet-snakes will leave the stone and impregnate the female carpet-snakes, thereby increasing the food supply.

Other informants claimed that the carpet-snake stones at Kuniapiti were somewhat different from increase stones elsewhere, for example, those of the sleepy-lizard (Pl. 96B). They explained that before the men went out hunting on a hot morning they rubbed the Kunia stones, chanting a special song. This ceremony, called *lurubunangi*, would wake up the life essence, *kurunba*, of carpet-snakes in the stone, which, in turn, would go out and cause the carpet-snakes to leave their holes and wander about, thus making it easier for the hunters to catch them. It is, of course, possible that both rituals are used, one for the increase of carpet-snakes and one for hunting magic.

The supposed efficacy of one or another of these rituals, or perhaps both, is shown by the fact that the rough surfaces of these stones have been rubbed practically smooth. Around the corner of the large boulder once forming the windbreak of the Kunia man and his wife there is a smooth shallow depression on the vertical face (Pl. 30A). At the same time as the aborigines perform the rituals on the Kunia stones, they rub the inside of this depression with a smooth boulder. This ritual, it is believed, will cause all the carpet-snakes in the country to grow large and fat.

PLATE 29. The carpet-snakes, Kunia: A, Totemic place of Kunia women, eastern Ayers Rock; B, Body of Kunia man, Ungata (increase centre for carpet-snakes).

PLATE 30. The carpet-snakes, Kunia: A, Boulder which, when rubbed, makes carpet-snakes fat; B, Body of Kunia woman, Ingridi (increase centre for carpet-snakes).

PLATE 31. The hare-wallaby, Mala woman, and poisonous snake, Liru man: A, Where Liru man raped Mala woman; B, Liru man (left) and Mala woman (right).

PLATE 32. The hare-wallaby, Mala woman, and poisonous-snake Liru man: A, Water-course where Liru man returned to companions on southern side; B, Track made by Mala people as they travelled to Ayers Rock.

PLATE 33. The hare-wallabies, Mala: A, Camp of Mala women; B, Camp of Mala women of the Tanamildjan moiety.

While the main body of the Liru were destroying the harmless carpet-snakes, two others, on mischief bent, travelled to the northern side of Uluru. One of them, angry because the woman Kunia Ingridi had killed his brother, Kulikudjeri, crept up to the camp of the willy-wagtail woman, Tjinderi-tjinderiba (the daughter of Kunia Ingridi, Fig. 3) to take his revenge. Waiting until the willy-wagtail woman was resting in the sun with her children, he cast a spear that passed completely through her body.[10]

The other Liru man caught and raped a hare-wallaby (Mala) woman as she was returning to camp with a load of firewood. The knee-marks which the Liru man made in the sand as he copulated are now a series of pot-holes in the stony surface (Pl. 31A). Near by are two small boulders (Pl. 31B), the transformed bodies of the man and woman sitting together after the incident. A black water-stain on the floor of a spectacular gorge (Pl. 32A), marks the track of the Liru man as he returned to his companions on the southern side.

After the Liru had completed their work of destruction at Uluru, they returned to Katatjuta and, joining forces with the giant Pungalunga men of that locality,[11] set out to destroy the harmless mythical snakes at Kunduna, in the Tomkinson Ranges of South Australia; but the Kunduna snakes were so well prepared and powerful that they destroyed every one of their attackers.

(*b*) *The Hare-wallabies, Mala, and the Spirit Dingo, Kulpunya*

At the same time as the carpet-snake people were making their camps at the Uluru waterhole on the south-eastern corner of Ayers Rock (Fig. 3), a party of hare-wallabies, the Mala (*Lagorchestes hirsutus*), left their camp at Marununga, an unlocalized place north-west of Mt Liebig, and travelled to Ayers Rock in order to pass their youths through the rites of circumcision and sub-incision. The route by which they approached Uluru is now an outcropping line of bare rock on the north-western corner (Pl. 32B).

The main camp of the Mala women and children is now a large cave, over four hundred yards long, formed by differential erosion on the north-western corner of the Rock (Pl. 33A and Fig. 3). This cave is divided naturally into three sections; the first section to the east (Pl. 34A) was once the camp of the *Nanandurak̦a* women;[12] the central section that of the *Tanamildjan* (Pl. 33B); and the most westerly section (Pl. 34B), the camp of Mala children

[10] Fuller details of the topography and beliefs associated with the willy-wagtail woman are included on p. 144.

[11] Mountford (1948, p. 96), gives a short description of the Pungalunga myth.

[12] As explained earlier, the Pitjandjara tribe is divided into two groups, i.e. the *Nananduraka* (my people), and *Tanamildjan* (others). For the purpose of clarity, the totemic places and groups will be referred to as they stand in relation to my Pitjandjara informant, Balinga.

PLATE 34. The hare-wallabies, Mala: A, Camp of women of the Nananduraka moiety; B, Camp of children of Mala women.

PLATE 35. The hare-wallabies, Mala: A, Lower camp of Mala children; B, Breasts of Mala women.

PLATE 36. The hare-wallabies, Mala: A, Boulders, once mother nursing sick child; B, Clitorides of Mala women.

Plate 37. The hare-wallabies, Mala, at Tabudja: A, Piles of food prepared by the Mala women of Tabudja; B, The totemic place of Tabudja.

PLATE 38. The hare-wallabies, Mala, at Tabudja: A, Lines of food ready to be gathered into heaps; B, Cleft in rock, once a digging stick of Mala woman.

of many ages. The erosion patterns on the cliff face, particularly on the central and westerly caves (Pl. 35A, B) symbolize the transformed breasts, and the curiously eroded fragments of rock hanging from the ceilings of the two easterly caves (Pl. 36B), the clitorides of the women. The large and small boulders scattered on the plain at the base of the women's cave (Pls 33, 34) were either Mala women and their children warming themselves in the sun, or their excreta. One particular group of boulders (Pl. 36A) is the transformed body of a woman holding a sick child in her arms.

While the initiation ceremonies were in progress at Ayers Rock, the men, to ensure the secrecy of their rituals, sent the women and children to Tabudja (Pl. 37B and Fig. 3), a low isolated hill near the eastern end of Uluru, where they gathered the yellow-fruited solanum, *yirtumba* (*Solanum coactiliferum*), from the surrounding flats, and cooked it in the ashes of their camp fire. The reefs of stone (Pl. 38A and Fig. 3) were once lines of *yirtumba* which the women had collected preparatory to cooking, and the low mounds of rock (Pl. 37A and Fig. 3), piles of cooked fruit ready to be taken back to the men for their evening meal. A transformed digging stick of one of the women is now a long cleft on the summit of Tabudja (Pl. 38B); the children who accompanied the Mala women to Tabudja, small boulders on the northern side (Pls 39A, 42A, 43A); the older women resting, rounded boulders on the summit of Tabudja (Pl. 39B); and the young women setting out to collect the *yirtumba* from the surrounding country, lines of standing boulders on the eastern end (Pl. 40B). The pubic hairs of the women, where they once sat on the summit of Tabudja have been transformed into tufts of grass that grow in the crevices (Pl. 40A).

On the southern slopes of Tabudja there is a low shallow cave (similar to that illustrated in Pl. 42B), which, during creation times, was the wet-weather shelter of the Mala nursing mothers. Their infants were transformed into small boulders on the floor of the cave (Pl. 41A), and the breasts of the mothers into curious erosion patterns on the back wall (Pl. 41B).

The transformed windbreak of the dry-weather camp of the other Mala women is now a long column of rock on the northern side of Tabudja (Pl. 43A), and the bodies of the Mala women sheltering behind it, the boulders at either end (Pls 39A, 44B).

At the base of Uluru, immediately south of Tabudja, an erosion cave (Pl. 45A and Fig. 3) was once the wet-weather shelter of an old Mala man whose duty it was to see that the Mala women did not leave their camp at Tabudja and spy on the initiation rituals of the men. The long boulder (Pl. 46B) at the mouth of this cave

Plate 39. The hare-wallabies, Mala, at Tabudja: A, Mala children in dry-weather camp; B, Older Mala women sitting down.

PLATE 40. The hare-wallabies, Mala, at Tabudja: A, Grass, once pubic hairs of Mala women; B, Boulders, once young Mala women standing up.

PLATE 41. The hare-wallabies, Mala, at Tabudja: A, Infants of Mala women in wet-weather shelter; B, Breasts of nursing Mala women in wet-weather shelter.

was once the old Mala man keeping watch on the women at Tabudja; the depressions in the rock near by (Pl. 46A), places where he had urinated during the night; and the small circular caves in an adjacent cliff (Pl. 45B), holes in his nasal septum in which he inserted a nose bone.

High up the face of Uluru, and immediately east of the camp of the old Mala man there are several pairs of circular caves (Pl. 44A). These were once holes which the old Mala man and his companions had dug in the ground so that they could perform a ceremony to pass away the time. The dark water-stain below these caves was the place where the men had danced; and the ledge immediately above, the windbreak behind which they once decorated themselves.

While the women at Tabudja were gathering their food under the watchful eye of the old Mala man (Pl. 46B), other men were carrying out the initiation ceremonies on the northern and north-western sides of Ayers Rock. Toward the summit and east of the main camp of the Mala women (Pl. 33A) are several extensively eroded areas (Pl. 47A, B and Fig. 3). The long curving lines of caves in the largest area (Pl. 47A) were once the initiates, lying on the ground, being decorated by the old Mala men. The camps of these old men are now the central eroded area of Pl. 47B; and the dark stain on the face of Uluru where the water from the summit falls into the Tjinindi rockhole beneath (Pl. 47A) was the bark brush which the old men used to paint the ceremonial designs on the bodies of the initiates. The eroded areas on the right of Pl. 47A (shown in greater detail in Pl. 47B) are the transformed camps of a number of tribesmen whose duty it was to guard a much-valued eagle-chick, Kudrun, which the Mala people often used in their rituals. As the initiation ceremonies were performed only during the cool hours of the morning and the evening, both the old men and the initiates slept in the middle of the day. The large boulders piled against the side of Uluru adjacent to the Tjinindi rockhole (Pl. 49A and Fig. 3) were once a number of tribal elders sleeping in their camp;[13] the groups of smaller boulders at the base of the Rock (Pl. 48B), represent the initiates; and the small circular caves in the adjacent cliff face (Pl. 48A), camps occupied by the initiates during the rainy weather. A large boulder on the left of Pl. 49B is the transformed body of one of the old men guarding the sleeping initiates, who can be seen as boulders in the distance (Fig. 3).

There are also boulders and trees on the western part of the

[13] The aborigines will, whenever possible, travel and hunt during the morning and evening, preferring to rest in the shade when the day is hot.

PLATE 42. The hare-wallabies, Mala, at Tabudja: A, Boulder, once child of Mala woman; B, Wet-weather shelter of Mala women.

PLATE 43. The hare-wallabies, Mala, at Tabudja: A, Mala women and children in dry-weather camp; B, Dry-weather windbreak of Mala women at Tabudja.

PLATE 44. The hare-wallabies, Mala, at Tabudja: A, Holes in cliff where Mala man danced; B, Mala women and children in dry-weather camp at Tabudja.

PLATE 45. The hare-wallabies, Mala, at Tabudja: A, Camp of old Mala man who guarded Mala women; B, Small caves, once holes in nose of Mala man for his nose-bone.

PLATE 46. The hare-wallabies, Mala, at Tabudja: A, Holes where Mala man once urinated; B, Boulder, once old Mala man, guarding the women of Tabudja.

PLATE 47. The hare-wallabies, Mala: A, General view, northern face of Ayers Rock (arrow indicates camps of old Mala men and initiates); B, Arrow indicates camps of old Mala men.

PLATE 48. The hare-wallabies, Mala: A, Small caves, once camps of Mala initiates; B, Boulders, Mala initiates asleep.

summit of Uluru, which were, in creation times, groups of initiates being guarded by the old men. Pl. 50A illustrates a number of initiates sleeping, while an old man (the tree) keeps watch; Pl. 51B, another group of sleeping initiates being watched by another old man (the tree on Pl. 50B); and the isolated boulders on Pls 52A, 53A, sleeping initiates being guarded by other old men (the rocks on Pl. 52B). An open space on the summit of Uluru (Pl. 72B) was at one time the camp of the young men; the mulga-trees (Pl. 51A), their spears; a long boulder (Pl. 53B), one of their spearthrowers; and a rockhole (Pl. 72A), the camp of one of the youths.

A decorated pole, the *naldawata,* around which many of the dances and rituals were performed, was erected in the middle of the ceremonial ground. This *naldawata* pole, with several sacred objects (*kulpidji*) hanging from a cross piece at the top, and decorated with designs in red, yellow and white down, appears to have been similar to the *nurtunja* poles (Pl. 106A) used by the Aranda tribe in their initiation ceremonies (see Spencer and Gillen, 1899, Figs 63, 64, 81, 86, and 88). At the close of the creation period, the *naldawata* pole was transformed into an immense slab of rock, a remarkable example of exfoliation, four to five hundred feet long (Pl. 54A), which is attached to the Rock at each end, and sprung away in the centre. Pl. 55A illustrates the gap between the base of the "pole" and the Rock. The old tribesmen responsible for the safe-keeping of the *naldawata* pole are now large spherical boulders near its base (Pl. 57A), and their camp, a low cave on the northern side (Pl. 56B). The old men who sheltered in this cave are now rocks at the entrance (Pl. 56A), and their hair, curious erosion patterns on the ceiling (Pl. 57B).

During *tjukurapa* times, the actual rituals of circumcision and sub-incision were performed on a patch of hard ground which was once the base of a termite mound.[14] The adult Mala men, after they had completed the surgical operations on the initiates, opened veins in their own arms, and allowed their blood to fall on this hard surface. At the close of the creation period, this hard surface was transformed into the back wall of a long cylindrical cave on the western side of Uluru (Pl. 58A and Fig. 3). From that time onward, the men of the Mala totem, both when they take part in the initiation rituals and when they pay a visit to Uluru, open the veins in their arms and allow the blood to pour over the back wall of this cave. When this cave was first visited in 1940, the wall, for most of its length, was covered with lines of blood from the arms

[14] An old termite mound, when it has been eroded to the level of the surrounding country, is so hard and dense that no grass or any other plant will grow on its surface.

PLATE 49. The hare-wallabies, Mala: A, Rocks, old Mala men asleep; B, Boulder on left, old Mala man guarding initiates (in distance).

PLATE 50. The hare-wallabies, Mala: A, Tree, once old man guarding initiates (boulders at base); B, Tree, old man guarding initiates (boulders on Plate 51B).

PLATE 51. The hare-wallabies, Mala: A, Mulga-trees, once spears of Mala men; B, Boulders, groups of sleeping initiates.

PLATE 52. The hare-wallabies, Mala: A, Boulders, old Mala men in foreground, initiates at back; B, Boulders, two old Mala men.

PLATE 53. The hare-wallabies, Mala: A, Boulders, once initiates, resting; B, Boulder, spearthrower of Mala man.

PLATE 54. The hare-wallabies, Mala: A, The *naldawata* (ceremonial pole) of Mala initiation ceremony; B, Ceremonial pole being carried away by Mala men.

PLATE 55. The hare-wallabies, Mala: A, Base of *naldawata* pole; B, *Naldawata* pole being carried away (southern side).

PLATE 56. The hare-wallabies, Mala: A, Boulder, once old man resting in camp while guarding *naldawata* pole; B, Cave, once camp of old men who guarded *na!dawata* pole.

PLATE 57. The hare-wallabies, Mala: A, Large boulders, once two old men in charge of *naldawata* pole; B, Eroded boulders on ceiling of cave, hair of old men.

of visiting tribesmen (Pl. 59B). In approximately the middle of the cave there is a black vertical line (in 1940 it was a circle), which divides the cave into the two fundamental divisions of the tribe, the *Nananduraka* and the *Tanamildjan*. The right-hand side of Pl. 59B is *Nananduraka* to my informant, Balinga, i.e. it belongs to his totemic group, and the left is *Tanamildjan*. Every Ayers Rock youth passes through the rites of sub-incision and circumcision on the end of the cave belonging to his side of the tribe, that is to him *Nananduraka*.

In this cave there is a long flat stone (Pl. 63A) on which the prostrate initiate is decorated with the traditional designs in red, yellow, black and white, before passing through the actual initiation rituals. There are several flat places (Pl. 63B) where the ochres have been ground for such a long period that the surfaces of the boulder have been rubbed almost smooth.[15] As it is unlikely that the initiation ceremonies would have been held more often than once a year,[16] it must have taken centuries, perhaps even several millenniums, for the abrasive action of the blocks of comparatively soft ochres to have smoothed the hard stone of Ayers Rock to such an extent.

The cave is absolutely forbidden to women. They are not even allowed to look in that direction when passing, because every natural feature, large and small, is associated with the initiation rituals of the long-distant past. A tall conical rock (Pl. 61A) and a large split boulder (Pl. 60A) were once tribal elders in charge of the initiation; small rounded boulders at the mouth of the cave (Pl. 60B), the initiates sleeping as they await their turn to pass through the rituals; the grass between the boulders, their pubic hairs; and the fig-trees among the rocks, their growing beards. Clinging precariously to a small cleft on a vertical face on the northern side of the Rock is a single bloodwood-tree (Pl. 62A). This is the transformed body of an old Mala tribesman calling the other participants of the rituals to the ceremony.[17] A large tree on a ledge, high over the top of the initiation cave (Pl. 62B), was once the same man calling the Mala people together for the second time. The same tribal elder is repre-

[15] There are similar abrasion marks, although not so distinct, on a boulder (Pl. 58B) in the cave of the mourning Kunia woman, Ingridi (Pl. 23A). These marks and the presence of cave paintings of unusual designs on the adjacent rocks, suggest that ceremonies, probably associated with initiation, were once performed in this place.

It seems likely that when these ceremonies were superseded, perhaps by those of the present day, the tribal elders established the belief (see p.54) that the Kunia cave and the area surrounding it (Fig. 3) was so impregnated with *arukwita*, the spirit of disease and death, that it was dangerous for anyone to go near. This belief once established, would of course, completely suppress any rituals previously held in the cave.

[16] Tindale (1935, pp.199-204) described a circumcision ceremony he witnessed in the southern Musgrave Ranges; and the writer has witnessed both circumcision and sub-incision ceremonies of a similar type belonging to the Ngadadjara tribe of the Warburton Ranges, Western Australia.

[17] This is made by calling in a high-pitched voice, at the same time vibrating the hand in front of the mouth.

PLATE 58. The hare-wallabies, Mala: A, Tjalarina inspects cave paintings of wallaby myth; B, Stone in Kunia Ingridi's Cave (Plate 23A) where youths were decorated.

PLATE 59. The hare-wallabies, Mala: A, Boulders, once old Mala men chanting initiation songs; B, Matinya (1940) in initiation cave.

PLATE 60. The hare-wallabies, Mala: A, Boulders, group of old men resting near initiation cave; B, Boulders, initiates asleep at initiation cave.

PLATE 61. The hare-wallabies, Mala: A, Tall boulder, tribal leader in initiation ceremony; B, Dead bush and water-stains, once body of tribal leader.

PLATE 62. The hare-wallabies, Mala: A, Tree, once old Mala man, calling initiates to ceremony; B, Trees, once old Mala men, taking part in ceremony.

sented for the third time on the northern end of the initiation cave (Pl. 61B). The small dead tree in the centre of the photograph was the beard of the old man; the rectangular black mark on the top of the photograph, a patch of black paint on his sternum; the white water marks immediately below, his body decorations; and similar markings on the lower right, his pubic hairs. Low boulders, on the plain (Pl. 59A) were once initiated men chanting songs for the rituals.

At the time when the Mala tribesmen were initiating their youths, the Windulka (mulga-seed) men of Kikingura (a large hill on the western end of the Petermann Ranges), sent their messenger, the bell-bird, Panpanpanala,[18] to Ayers Rock to invite the Mala men and women to take part in one of their ceremonies and to ask them to bring their eagle-chick, Kudrun, with them so that they could use some of its down to decorate their actors.[19] When Panpanpanala delivered the invitation, and the message about their eagle-chick, the Mala tribesmen became so angry over the preposterous request that instead of eagle-down, they sent both a parcel of white ash and a discourteous reply saying that they did not have the slightest intention of lending their much-prized Kudrun just to supply eagle-down for people who were too lazy to hunt for their own, nor would they consider curtailing their own initiation ceremonies just to attend those of other people in which they were not interested.

This insolent message so annoyed the mulga-seed men that they instructed their medicine men to create a malignant spirit dingo, called Kulpunya, who would not only destroy the eagle-chick, Kudrun, but also its owners, the hare-wallaby people.

The medicine-men were soon busy on their task. After they had laid out the skeletal framework—a mulga branch for a backbone, forked sticks for ears, the teeth of a small marsupial mole at one end, the tail of a bandicoot at the other and women's hair along the back—they spent the rest of the day chanting songs of magic to fill Kulpunya with the spirit of evil. Then, from sunset to sunrise, they left it alone, for it is only during the hours of darkness that such a creature can develop.

The following morning, Kulpunya was showing signs of life; the hair was already growing along its back, the teeth had increased in size, and the feet were sprouting. Again, the medicine-men sat around their evil creation and chanted songs so effective

[18] Panpanpanala is now a pointed rock (Pl. 70A) on the southern side, near the camp of the sleepy-lizard (Fig. 3).

[19] Eagle-chicks are covered with a thick growth of white down. They are the main source of supply for down used in the ceremonies.

PLATE 63. The hare-wallabies, Mala: A, Stone in initiation cave on which youths were decorated; B, Close-up of grinding marks on stone above.

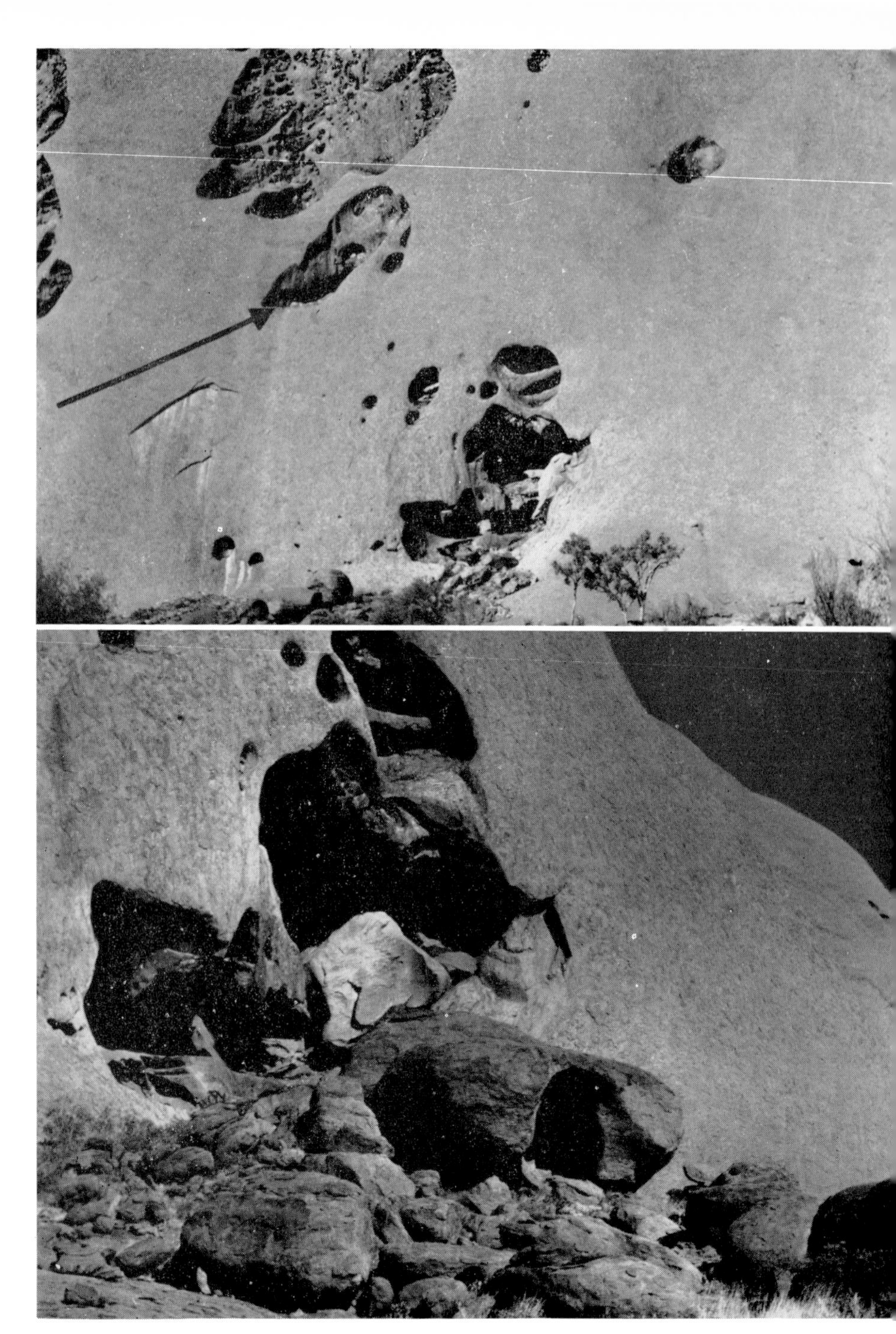

PLATE 64. The red-backed kingfisher-woman, Lunba: A, Cave at X (see arrow) from which Lunba watched for spirit dingo, Kulpunya; B, Boulders, where Lunba sat in front of her camp.

PLATE 65. The red-backed kingfisher-woman, Lunba: A, Camp of kingfisher-woman, Lunba; B, Upper projections in cave, breasts of Lunba.

PLATE 66. The red-backed kingfisher-woman, Lunba: A, Boulders where Lunba once rested in the sun; B, Boulders on summit, once Lunba; small caves, where she camped.

PLATE 67. The spirit dingo, Kulpunya: A, Ears and earhole of Kulpunya; B, Kulpunya after arrival from Kikingura.

that through the next night it had actually crawled some distance. Next morning the medicine-men brought the creature back to camp and chanted the final songs to fill it with hatred and malice towards all strangers. When Kulpunya was fully grown, the mulga-seed men ordered it to go to Ayers Rock on its diabolical mission. The creature was about the size of a dingo, but had no hair on its body except along its back and the point of its tail. The transplanted teeth had grown to a formidable size and its malevolence had increased exceedingly. Meanwhile, the Mala people of Ayers Rock were following their way of life, the men performing the initiation ceremonies for their youths, and the women at Tabudja collecting and preparing food for them.

There was, however, an old kingfisher woman *Lunba*, who, expecting an attack from the mulga-seed people of Kikingura, had made her camps apart from the other women so that, by getting a better view of the surrounding country, she could warn the Mala people should she see anyone approaching.

Along the northern face of Uluru there are a number of caves (Pls 64A, B, 65A, B, and Fig. 3) which were, in creation times, places where Lunba had made her camps. A boulder at the opening of the cave in Pl. 66A is the transformed body of Lunba where she had once rested in the sun. The two projections from the roof (Pl. 65B) are her breasts.

When the Mala people were having their mid-day rest, it was Lunba's custom to sit under the shade of a tree and keep watch. At the close of the creation period this tree was transformed into a cave high up the Rock, and Lunba into a low bush[20] in the lower left-hand corner (Pl. 64A).

When, at mid-day, Kulpunya reached Ayers Rock, everyone with the exception of Lunba was asleep. Kulpunya paused to see that the women were asleep in their main camp (Pl. 33A) before he sneaked along the northern face. Today there is a large conical boulder (Pl. 67B) at the place, the small cavities in the top (Pl. 67A) being Kulpunya's ear and earhole.

Kulpunya was immediately under the camp of Lunba (Pl. 64A) when he raised his head[21] to see where the Mala men kept their treasured eagle-chick, Kudrun. This movement attracted the attention of Lunba, who quickly gave the alarm. On hearing this, Kulpunya, running quickly along the ground, paused first at the wet-weather camp of the willy-wagtail women (Pl. 102A), where today

[20] When I visited Ayers Rock in both 1935 and 1940, there was a large bloodwood-tree in the same position as this bush. When later this tree died, or was blown over by a storm, the aborigines obviously transferred the myth to the small bush.

[21] A slab of rock immediately underneath this place (Pl. 68A) symbolizes Kulpunya looking upwards.

PLATE 68. The spirit dingo, Kulpunya: A, Vertical boulder, once Kulpunya creeping up to attack Mala people; B, Paired caves in cliff, footmarks of Kulpunya as he attacked and killed eagle-chick, Kudrun (see arrow).

PLATE 69. The spirit dingo, Kulpunya: A, Tree at Tjinindi rockhole, once Kulpunya; B, Boulder, Kulpunya at camp of willy-wagtail woman.

PLATE 70. The spirit dingo, Kulpunya: A, Stone, body of bell-bird, Panpanpanala; B, Kulpunya, at Tjinindi rockhole, ready to attack the Mala people.

PLATE 71. The hare-wallabies, Mala: A, Gutters on summit formed when Mala men dragged *naldawata* pole to safety; B, Gutters on summit made by feet of running Mala men.

PLATE 72. The hare-wallabies, Mala: A, Camp of young Mala man; B, Open space, camp of young and old Mala men.

there is a spectacular slab of rock (Pl. 69B); then he ran on to the Tjinindi rockhole, where a bloodwood-tree (Pl. 69A) and a long column of rock (Pl. 70B) mark the places where he paused again before he crept up to Kudrun's camp and destroyed the chick by tearing its body in two pieces. Balinga, my informant, pointed out pairs of circular caves in the steep face of Uluru, which he said were once the footmarks of Kulpunya (Pl. 68B), and two white marks on the top of the cliff which symbolize the dismembered body of Kudrun. This task accomplished, Kulpunya attacked and destroyed all the women and children in their main camp (Pl. 33A), the women preparing the food at Tabudja (Pl. 37B), and the old men and the initiates adjacent to the Tjinindi rockhole (Pls 48, 49).

When Lunba, the kingfisher woman, realized that her efforts to save the Mala on the northern face were unsuccessful, she ran quickly to the western side of Uluru and warned the adult men and the initiates of their danger. Lunba's body is now a large boulder on the western margin of the summit of Uluru (Pl. 66B), and her camps, small circular caves near at hand. On hearing Lunba's warning the Mala men, who were performing the initiation ceremonies on the western side of the Rock, quickly assembled, and taking the *naldawata* pole from the ceremonial ground, gave it to the initiates to drag to safety. The footmarks of the young men as they dragged the pole away are now spectacular chasms on the north-western corner of Uluru (Pl. 54B), and the immense column of rock lying between them (Pls 54B, 55B), the transformed *naldawata* pole. The feet of the Mala initiates also made deep gutters on the summit as they dragged the ceremonial pole from the north-west to the south-east of the Rock (Pl. 71A). Other gutters (Pl. 71B) were created by the feet of the Mala men as they fled from Kulpunya (Fig. 3).

The Mala men, the initiates dragging the *naldawata* pole, accompanied by the kingfisher woman, Lunba, fled eastward to Mt Sir Henry and a spring called Oolra (obviously the same name as Uluru), which is adjacent to Mt Cavanagh station, on the south and central Australian border. According to Balinga, the whole myth was being re-enacted when Kulpunya followed and again attacked the Mala people.

(*c*) *The Lizard-men, Kandju and Linga*

At the time these incidents were taking place at Ayers Rock, a little lizard-man, Kandju, lived by himself in an unidentified place west of Uluru. One day, when trying out a boomerang he had just made, the weapon rose high into the air and, spinning horizontally,

PLATE 73. The lizard, Kandju: A, The totemic place of the lizard, Kandju; B, Kandju water, dry-weather camp of the lizard, Kandju.

PLATE 74. The lizard, Kandju: A, Gutters and holes dug by Kandju in search of lost boomerang; B, Cave, wet-weather camp of Kandju.

Plate 75. The lizard, Kandju: A, Cave, once tree, where Kandju sheltered from sun; B, Long boulder, once Kandju's spear-thrower.

PLATE 76. The lizard, Kandju: A, Erosion on ceiling, leaves of tree under which Kandju slept; B, Large boulders where Kandju slept.

PLATE 77. The lizard, Linga: A, Curving edge of rockhole, once Kandju's boomerang; B, Erosion in back of large cave, once places where ants bit Linga.

buried itself in the soft sand of Uluru.[22] Greatly distressed over his loss, Kandju travelled quickly to Uluru, which was many miles away, and dug everywhere with his bare hands until he found it. Many of the spectacular topographical features in the Kandju gorge (Pl. 73A and Fig. 3) on the western side of the present Ayers Rock are the result of Kandju's frantic search in the sand for his lost boomerang. The deep holes and gutters which Kandju dug in the sand have since been transformed into either deep pot-holes or vertical chasms in the steep precipices of this beautiful gorge (Pls 73A, 74A), and the boomerang into the curving edge of one of the larger pot-holes (Pl. 77A).

Having found his missing weapon, the lizard-man decided to stay in this locality for a while. His dry-weather camp is now the Kandju waterhole (Pl. 73B); his beard, a black mark at the head of the gorge made by the falling water (Pl. 73A); and his wet-weather camp, a small erosion cave near by (Pl. 74B). There is a large cave on the northern side of Kandju gorge (Pl. 75A), which, during creation times, was a tree under which Kandju often rested. The large boulders at the mouth of the cave (Pl. 76B) symbolize places where Kandju slept; a horizontal column of rock (Pl. 75B), the place where he left his spearthrower; and the long curving vertical cleft (Pls 73A, 75A), which extends from ground level to the summit, Kandju's spear which he had leant against the tree before he went to sleep. The aborigines also believe that the curiously eroded rocks that hang from the ceiling of the cave (Pl. 76A) are the transformed leaves of the tree under which Kandju slept, and the fig-trees that grow among the boulders, his hair (Pl. 76B).

After a while, Kandju moved to the northern side of Uluru, near Tabudja, the camp of the Mala women (Pl. 37B). In this section of the myth, the aborigines referred to the lizard-man as Linga even though they were definite that Kandju and Linga were the same person.[23]

While in this locality, Linga lived entirely on honey-ants (*Melophorus inflatus*), insects which still provide the present-day aborigines with their major source of sweet food.[24] But when Linga

[22] As mentioned earlier, Uluru was, in creation times, a large sandhill.

[23] Later, the aborigines brought me a small lizard, about seven inches long (*Amphibolurus reticulatus*), which, they said, had three names, i.e. *Kandju*, *Linga* and *Tabuda*. The aborigines could not explain why, in the Ayers Rock myths, Kandju on the western side had been changed to Linga on the northern side. Tabuda is also associated with a myth belonging to Mt Conner. More research is needed to unravel this problem.

[24] Spencer and Gillen (1912, p.122), when describing these ants, write: "In the next we dug, there are two kinds of ants, one (the workers) for the ordinary tasks and the other, the honey ant. The latter is a remarkable modification of certain members of a social colony to serve a special purpose. . . . Instead of storing honey in combs as a reserve supply of food, when it is otherwise scarce, the ants use certain members of their own colony for the same purpose. The special insect is fed with honey until its abdomen, in which the honey is stored, becomes enormously distended. . . . When the ants wish to take advantage of this supply of food, it is said that they tap the swollen abdomen with their feet. . . ."

PLATE 78. The lizard, Linga: A, General view, northern face, showing camps of Linga (arrow indicates Linga's last camp); B, Close-up of wounds on Linga's body, caused by ant bites (in cave, Plate 77B).

Plate 79. The lizard, Linga: A, Third camp of Linga, on northern side of Ayers Rock: B, Second camp of Linga, boulders in front where Linga rested.

PLATE 80. The lizard, Linga: A, Fourth camp of Linga; B, Long boulder, once the digging-stick of Linga.

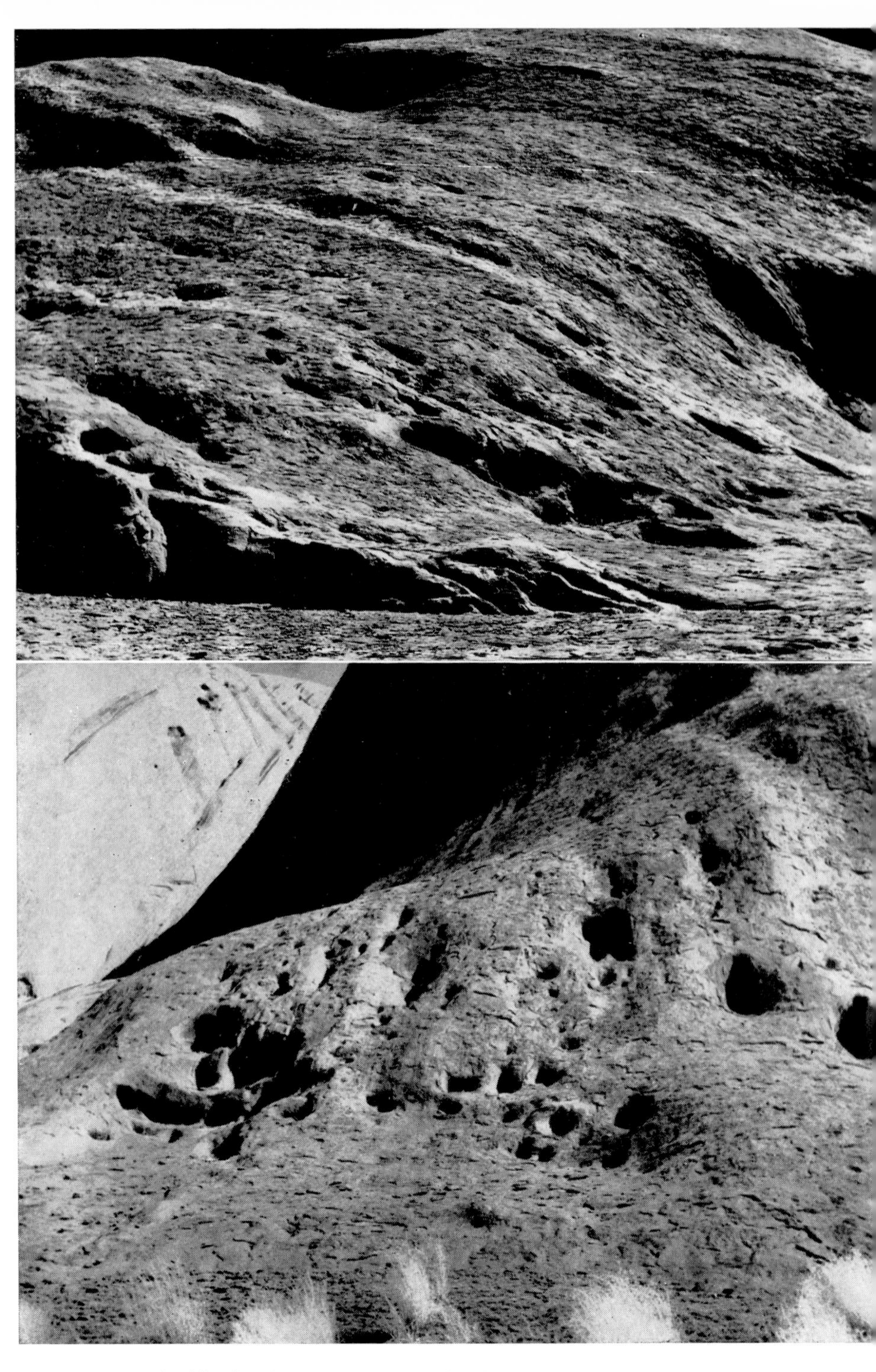

PLATE 81. The lizard, Linga: A, Footmarks of Linga as he crept up to kill Kunia woman; B, Holes in rock where Linga stood to kill woman.

PLATE 82. The lizard, Linga: A, Rock strata, once track made by Linga as he dragged murdered Kunia to his camp on summit; B, Details of rock below; C, Rock, once body of murdered Kunia woman.

dug out the honey-ants to get a meal, the worker ants of the colony followed him to his camp and bit him so severely that he was forced to leave one camp after another. There are now four large caves more or less at ground level (Pls 77B, 79A, B, 80A, and Fig. 3) out of which the lizard-man was driven by the marauding ants. In desperation, Linga established a camp (Pl. 78A) some distance from the others, but the ants still followed and tormented him so much that he moved to the southern face of Uluru.

Linga, being unable to find honey-ants or any other kind of food at his new camp, became so hungry that he almost starved to death. One day, when returning from an unsuccessful search for food, he saw a young carpet-snake girl asleep in front of her wet-weather shelter. Desperately hungry, he sneaked up with a digging stick and killed her with a heavy blow across her neck. The tracks Linga made as he crept up to his victim are now shallow depressions on a pavement at the base of the southern side of Ayers Rock (Pl. 81A); the spot where he stood to deliver the final blow, a series of pot-holes (left of Pl. 81B); and his digging stick, a long column of stone (Pl. 80B) in one of the northerly caves (Pl. 79A). The body of the Kunia girl has since been changed into a curiously-shaped boulder at ground level (Pl. 82C); the wound in her neck into the fissure at the top of the boulder; and her wet-weather camps, into small circular caves close at hand. The mythological details of the boulder are shown in Pl. 82B.

After having killed the unfortunate Kunia girl, Linga, dragging her corpse behind him, laid her out near his camp while he prepared the fire for cooking. The track made by Linga as he dragged the body is now a low ridge of rock extending from the ground to the summit of Uluru (Pl. 82A); Linga's camp, a pile of large boulders on top (Pl. 83A); and the body of his victim, a line of stones in the distance. After having cooked the body of the Kunia girl, Linga dismembered it in readiness for his gruesome meal. The camp fire has since been transformed into a circular rockhole on the summit (Pl. 84A); the shoulders and head of the Kunia girl into spherical rocks (Pl. 83B); and the legs and body into long cylindrical boulders (Pl. 84B).

His hunger satisfied, the lizard-man, Linga, left Uluru and travelled to Junabidi (unlocalized) on the southern side of the Musgrave Ranges, after which my informants had no further knowledge of him.

(*d*) *The Marsupial Moles, Itjari-tjari*

The marsupial moles, Itjari-tjari, at present small burrowing creatures

PLATE 83. The lizard, Linga: A, Boulders, camp of Linga on summit; line of stones in distance, body of dead Kunia woman; B, Head and shoulders of dead Kunia woman.

PLATE 84. The lizard, Linga: A, Rockhole where Linga cooked the murdered Kunia woman; B, Rocks, legs of Kunia woman.

PLATE 85. The marsupial moles, Itjari-tjari: A, Holes on western side of Ayers Rock dug by Itjari-tjari in search of food; B, Small wet-weather shelter of Itjari-tjari.

PLATE 86. The marsupial moles, Itjari-tjari: A, Dry-weather shelter of Itjari-tjari (note man in foreground); B, Dry-weather shelter in distance and holes dug by Itjari-tjari in search of food.

PLATE 87. The marsupial moles, Itjari-tjari: A, Wet-weather shelter of Itjari-tjari; B, Large boulder with rockhole in summit, once carrying dish of Itjari-tjari women.

(*Notoryctes typhlops*) little more than four inches in length, lived, during *tjukurapa* times, in and around their totemic place immediately south of Kandju gorge (Fig. 3). Here they followed their own peaceful way of life, burrowing in the soft sand for their food during the day, and sleeping in their camps at night, neither disturbed by the warring snakes to the south, nor the attacks of Kulpunya on the unfortunate hare-wallaby people to the north of them.

At the close of the creation period, the holes which the little people had dug in the sand became large pot-holes in the steep sides of Ayers Rock (Pl. 85A), and their dry-weather camp, a huge bowl high up the side of Uluru (Pl. 86A). This bowl is enclosed on three sides by a high curving precipice, which in *tjukurapa* times was a windbreak of boughs (Pl. 86A).

The wet-weather shelters which the marsupial mole people constructed of boughs and grass to keep out the rain, are now two caves at ground level, the small boulders lying at the mouth of the most southerly of them (Pl. 85B) being, at one time, the excreta of the marsupial moles. The other wet-weather shelter (Pl. 87A) is an attractive exfoliation cave. The footmarks of the marsupial mole people are now light-coloured marks on the floor of the cave (Pl. 88B); and the boulders projecting from the ceiling the noses, and the curving lines the beards of the men (Pl. 89A). The protuberances on the back wall of the cave symbolize the breasts, and the lines above (Pl. 89B) the hair, of the women. On the top of a large isolated boulder near the wet-weather shelters (Pl. 87B) is a depression that holds water for a considerable time after rain. This boulder, according to the mythical story, was once a wooden carrying dish in which the marsupial mole women brought water to the camp.

(*e*) *The Man and Woman, Kadidi*

The totemic place of *wati* and *minma* Kadidi, (wati—man; minma—married woman) consists of a series of large tor-like boulders (Pl. 90A and Fig. 3) to the west of the place of the marsupial moles. This couple, like their neighbours the moles, lived their own peaceful life at Uluru, neither disturbing nor being disturbed by anyone.

Their wet-weather shelter (Pl. 91A), which had been made of branches of mulga and grass, is now a large dry cave; the fig-trees on top, Kadidi's hair; the short grass at the base, her pubic hairs; and the boulders near by (Pl. 90A), her dogs. The wooden carrying dishes which the woman had placed on the top of the wet-weather shelter have since been changed into holes in the large boulder (Pl. 91A), and the grass-seed which she had collected and spread

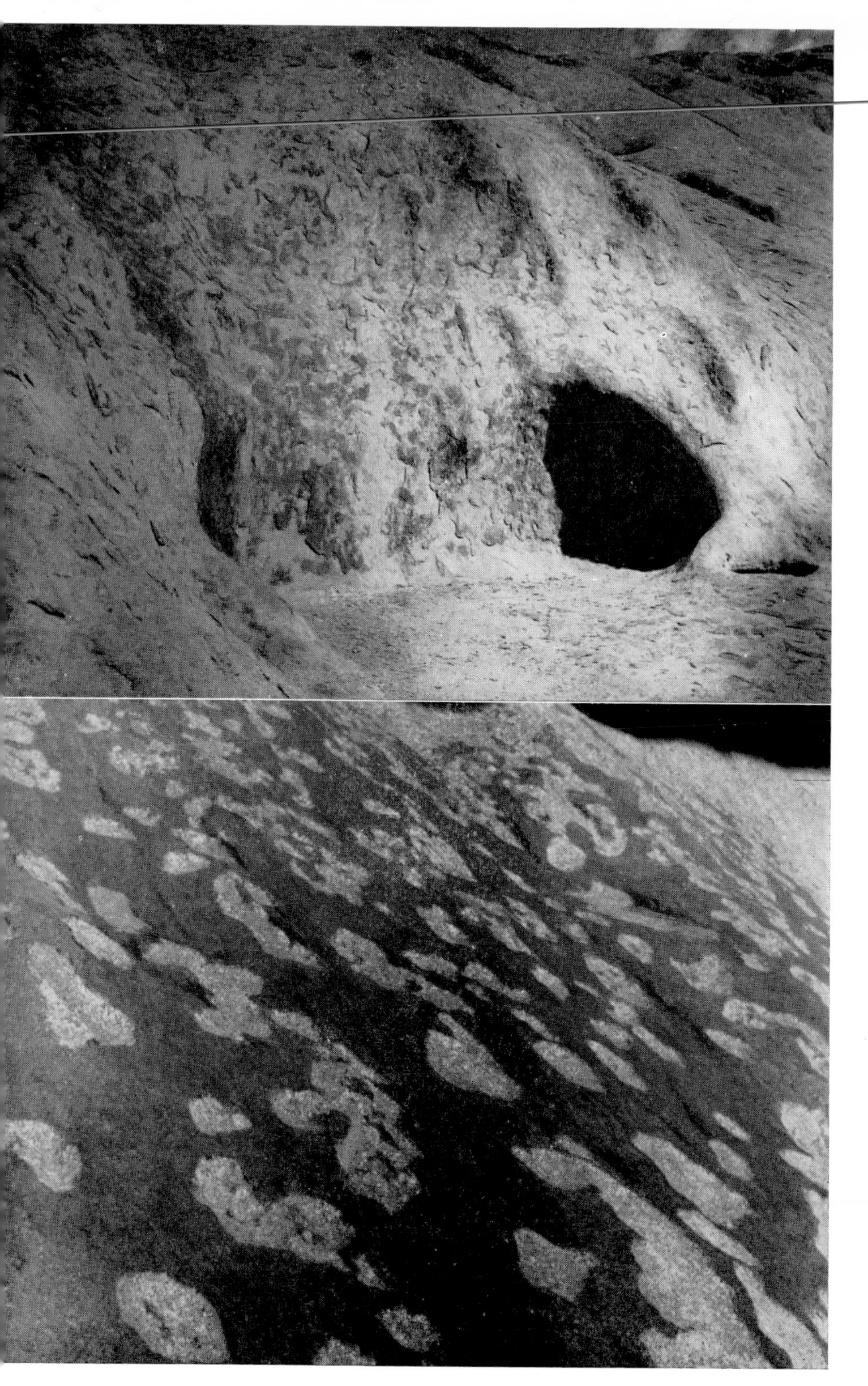

Plate 88. The marsupial moles, Itjari-tjari: A, Place on summit where Itjari-tjari rested; B, Footmarks of marsupial moles on floor of cave (Plate 87A).

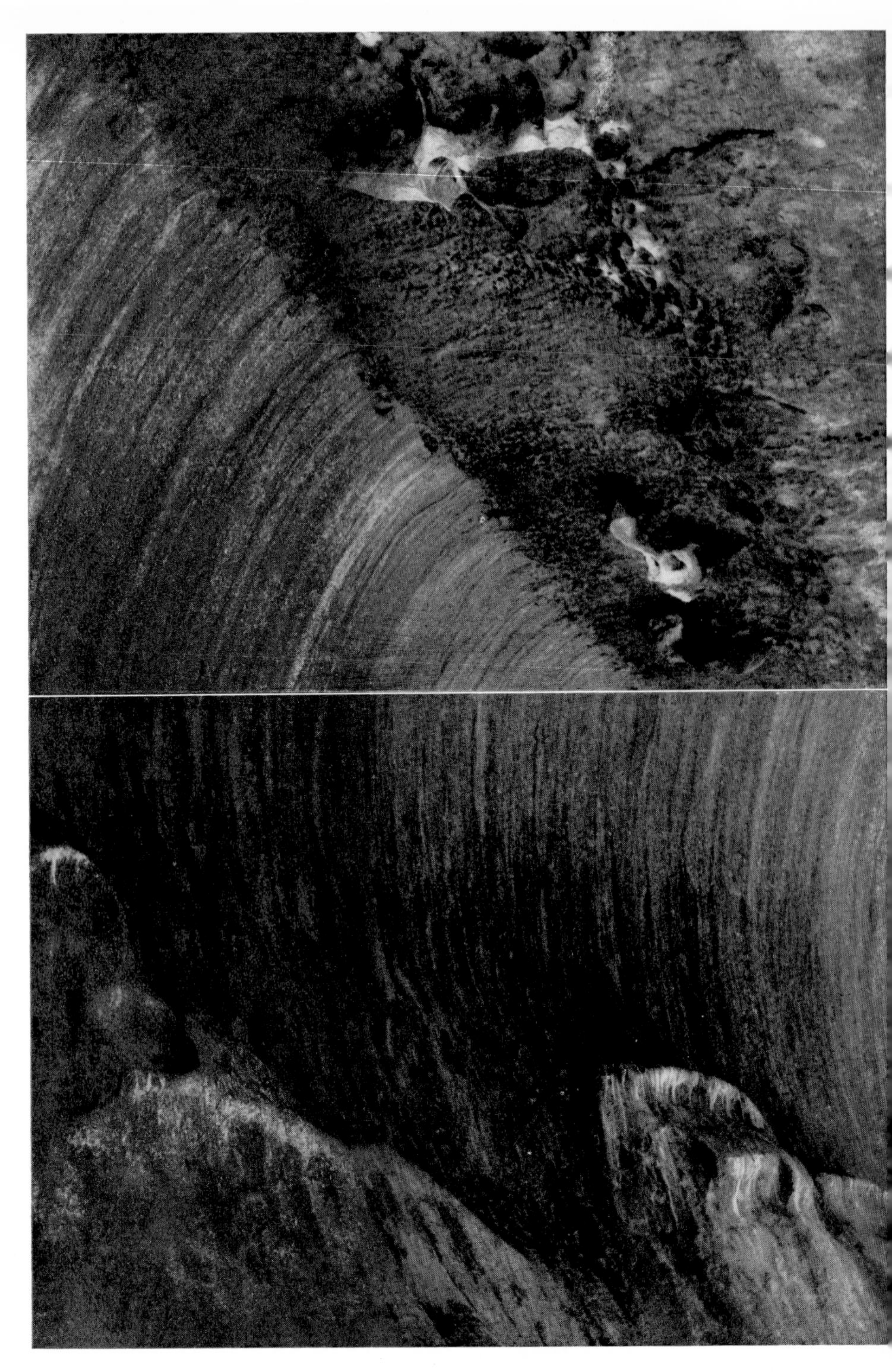

PLATE 89. The marsupial moles, Itjari-tjari: A, Erosion on ceiling, once whiskers of marsupial mole men; B. Protuberances on wall of cave, breasts of Itjari-tjari women.

PLATE 90. The man and woman, Kadidi: A, totemic place of man and woman, Kadidi; B, Caves, once places where couple rested in the sun.

PLATE 91. The man and woman, Kadidi: A, Wet-weather camp of man and woman, Kadidi; B, Boulders, once carrying dishes and piles of grass seed collected by the woman, Kadidi.

PLATE 92. The sleepy-lizard, Meta-lungana: A, Vertical pillar, once lower spine of dismembered emu; B, Rockhole, Kalaia-tjunda, where sleepy-lizard man cooked emu.

out for final winnowing and grinding, into masses of rock on the extreme south-western corner of Ayers Rock (Pl. 91B). The two shallow caves (Pl. 90B) in a smaller boulder to the east of the wet-weather camp (Pl. 90A) were once depressions in the sand where the mythical man and woman sat, Kadidi to the left and her husband to the right.

(*f*) *The Sleepy-lizard man, Meta-lungana*

During *tjukurapa* times, an unmarried sleepy-lizard man, called Meta-lungana (*Tiliqua scincoides*), lived by himself at Uluru. Meta-lungana was a particularly mean fellow, and never once—although it is a fundamental law among the aborigines to do so—did he share any of the meat he had caught with his neighbours, the carpet-snake people. He would leave his hunting camp, now a rock-hole in the Metjan gorge (Pl. 93B and Fig. 3), and travel into the desert country south of Uluru to hunt for emus. If he was successful, he would wait until after dark before he brought the dead bird back to camp. Early next morning, Meta-lungana would cook the bird in his camp fire (Pl. 92B), sometimes immediately dismembering the body and hiding the parts under low bushes near at hand.

At the close of the creation period, Meta-lungana's cooking place became a small rockhole, Kalaia-tjunda (emu-leg) (Pl. 92B and Fig. 3); the vertical black line above the rockhole, the gutter which Meta-lungana made as he dragged the cooked emu from the fire; and the small pot-holes in the vertical face, the metamorphosed knee-marks which the sleepy-lizard man made as he hid the meat under a low bush. This bush has since been transformed into a small cave. A tall pillar of rock (Pl. 92A) was once the lower part of the emu's backbone; a shallow cave, high up the Rock, one of its legs (Pl. 93A); and a long somewhat cylindrical boulder at ground level (Pl. 97A), the other leg. Although the sleepy-lizard man cooked all the emus he had speared at his cooking fire (Pl. 92B), he did not always dismember them immediately, sometimes preferring to carry the whole bird to his wet-weather shelter on the south-western corner of Uluru (Pl. 94A and Fig. 3), where he cut it up with his stone knife and hid the pieces in the bushes of his camp.

After a while, the carpet-snake people, becoming angry over the extreme meanness of their neighbour, pointed out to him that, by the tribal law, he should distribute a proportion of the emu he had caught among them, because some having large families were often hungry. But to this suggestion the sleepy-lizard man replied, in a sarcastic tone, that if the Kunia men were not clever enough

PLATE 93. The sleepy-lizard, Meta-lungana: A, Erosion pattern on southern side of Ayers Rock, once leg of dismembered emu; B, Metjan waterhole, dry-weather camp of sleepy-lizard.

Plate 94. The sleepy-lizard, Meta-lungana: A, Long cave, wet-weather camp of sleepy-lizard; B, Large area of lichen on southern Ayers Rock, once smoke from burning camp of sleepy-lizard. Arrow points to cave, once camp of sleepy-lizard.

Plate 95. The sleepy-lizard, Meta-lungana: A, Split boulders, once dismembered emu, and caves above, places where emu flesh was stored; B, Close-up of split boulders, once body of dismembered emu.

PLATE 96. The sleepy-lizard, Meta-lungana: A, The living sleepy-lizard, Meta-lungana; B, Boulders, once dead body of sleepy-lizard, now increase centre for these reptiles.

PLATE 97. The sleepy-lizard, Meta-lungana: A, Long boulder, once leg of emu: B, Cave painting illustrating emu hunt by sleepy-lizard man.

to get ample food for themselves and their families, he could see no reason why he should provide for them.

This reply so enraged the carpet-snake men that they decided to kill Meta-lungana. Waiting until he was lying asleep under a windbreak of boughs outside his wet-weather camp (Pl. 94A), the Kunia men crept up and set fire to it. The dense smoke overwhelmed Meta-lungana, and he rolled into the flames and died in agony.

The windbreak under which the sleepy-lizard man was sleeping is now a small cave near the summit of Uluru (Pl. 94B); the smoke from the burning camp, an extensive area of lichen on the southern side of Ayers Rock (Pl. 94B); the body of the dismembered emu, a large flat boulder, broken into many pieces (Pl. 95A, B); the hiding-places of the emu meat, small caves above the dismembered emu in Pl. 95A; Meta-lungana's wet-weather camp, a long cave on the southern face (Pl. 94A); and the dead body of Meta-lungana, a low rounded boulder at the base of Ayers Rock (Pl. 96B).

The aborigines look on this boulder, which they believe is full of the *kurunba* (life essence) of sleepy-lizards, as an increase centre for these reptiles. When, at the correct season, an aboriginal rubs this stone with another boulder—to the accompaniment of the correct chant—the *kurunba* of sleepy-lizards will leave the stone and impregnate the female sleepy-lizards who, by giving birth to their young, will increase the food supplies of the aborigines.

There is a cave painting of the sleepy-lizard myth on the right-hand side of a small cave at the home of the carpet-snake woman, Bulari (Pl. 97B, Fig. 3). The aborigines explained that the design on the bottom of the painting represents the dry-weather camp of Meta-lungana at the Metjan gorge (Pl. 93B). The details of the design illustrating the wet-weather camp are indicated by an inset in Fig. 33c. The Metjan waterhole is shown at a, the leg of the emu at b, Meta-lungana's windbreak at c and the body of the emu, indicated by its footprints, at d. One day Meta-lungana went out hunting (right-hand set of footmarks) and speared an emu, which ran away to the right, dragging the spear with it (full line indicates the mark made in the ground by the dragging spear). The splash of white paint on the upper right of the painting symbolizes the place where the lizard-man caught and killed the emu, which he put on his head and carried back to camp, where it was cooked. The left-hand set of footmarks indicate the return journey.

(g) *The Willy-wagtail Woman, Tjinderi-tjinderiba*

At the same time as the other totemic creatures were establishing themselves at Uluru, a mythical willy-wagtail woman, Tjinderi-

PLATE 98. The willy-wagtail woman, Tjinderi-tjinderiba: A, Rock-markings, once scars on arm of willy-wagtail woman; B, Tjinindi rockhole, once dry-weather camp of willy-wagtail woman.

Plate 99. The willy-wagtail woman, Tjinderi-tjinderiba: A, Long boulder, once body of willy-wagtail woman; B, Liru man preparing to spear Tjinderi-tjinderiba.

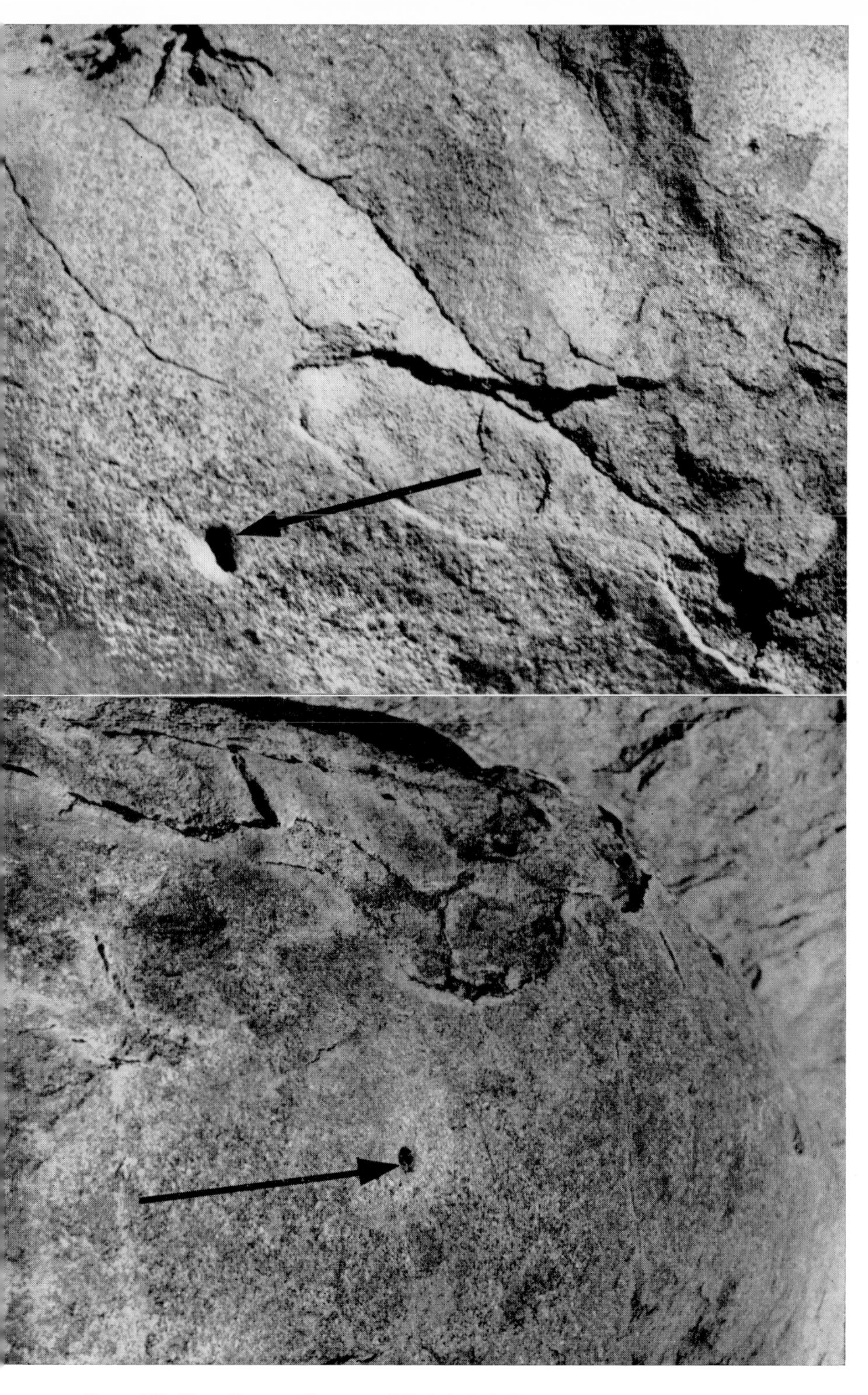

PLATE 100. The willy-wagtail woman, Tjinderi-tjinderiba: A, Hole (see arrow) where spear thrown by Liru entered woman's body; B, Place where spear emerged.

tjinderiba (*Rhipidura leucophrys*), with her many children, made a dry-weather camp on the northern side of Uluru (Fig. 3). At the close of *tjukurapa* times, the camp was transformed into the present-day Tjinindi rockhole (Pl. 98B), and its windbreak of boughs into the high cliff behind it.

About thirty yards west of Tjinindi rockhole is a long cylindrical boulder (Pl. 99A), the metamorphosed body of Tjinderi-tjinderiba, who had been speared by a Liru snake-man because her mother, Kunia Ingridi, had killed his brother, Kulikudjeri.[25] At one side of this boulder is a small hole (Pl. 100A) where the spear thrown by the Liru man had entered her body, and on the opposite side another hole (Pl. 100B) where it had emerged. At the same side of the boulder are a number of circular marks of human handiwork (Pl. 98A)[26] which, the aborigines explained, were once scars on the arms of Tjinderi-tjinderiba.[27] Adjacent to the body of the willy-wagtail woman is a smooth sloping surface on which, in creation times, the children of Tjinderi-tjinderiba amused themselves by sliding down on a pad of leaves. Balinga, my informant, who had also played this game as a boy, showed me how it was done (Pl. 101B).

There is a tumbled pile of large boulders (Pl. 102A) about fifty yards west of the totemic body of Tjinderi-tjinderiba. A shallow cave on the westerly side of this group was once the wet-weather camp of the willy-wagtail woman and her numerous children. Some of these, the well-grown children, are now large boulders (Pls 101A, 103A); younger children, as smaller boulders, are near the dead body of Tjinderi-tjinderiba (Pl. 99A), and her infants, of which there are four, small boulders at the back of a short tunnel (Pl. 104A) in the wet-weather camp (Pl. 102A).

In an adjacent shallow cave there is a small wall of stones from which there is a long white stain caused by running water (Pl. 104B). The wall was once a bough shelter behind which the infants slept, and the white line, their urine. Another white stain, originating in the cave of the four infants (Pl. 104A), has a similar meaning. On a level pavement outside the cave of these four infants are many shallow oval depressions (Pl. 103B), which, the aborigines believe, are the transformed marks which the infants made during *tjukurapa* times when they crawled about in the soft sand of Uluru.

The four boulders in this cave, the infants of Tjinderi-tjinderiba,

[25] There is a short account of this incident on p. 68.

[26] These small holes, and the adjacent circular carvings are the result of human handiwork. It is likely (although I have no evidence) that they would have played some part in the totemic rituals of the willy-wagtail woman.

[27] These scars are similar to those which the aboriginal girls delight in burning with small firesticks on the skins of their arms.

PLATE 101. The willy-wagtail woman, Tjinderi-tjinderiba: A, Boulders, once large and small children of willy-wagtail woman; B, Rock slide used by mythical children.

Plate 102. The willy-wagtail woman, Tjinderi-tjinderiba: A, Wet-weather camp of willy-wagtail woman; B, Grass, once pubic hairs of willy-wagtail woman.

PLATE 103. The willy-wagtail woman, Tjinderi-tjinderiba: A, Large boulders in foreground, once elder children of Tjinderi-tjinderiba; B, Depressions on rock surface where infants belonging to Tjinderi-tjinderiba once crawled in the sand.

contain an inexhaustible supply of spirit children, the *yulanya*, little beings only a few inches high, with light skin and long black hair. When one of these little people desires to become a human baby, it leaves its *yulanya* stone and sets out on a search for a suitable mother. On seeing a woman with large breasts and a kindly face whom it thinks would make a good mother, it quietly follows her and, waiting until she sits down or goes to sleep, enters her body through the vulva and starts life as a human being. The two right-hand boulders in the small cave (Pl. 104A) are *Tanamildjan* (the opposite moiety) from those on the left, and, of course, *Nanandura*k*a* (the same moiety) to each other. This position, as explained earlier, is reciprocal (p.19). A *yulanya* spirit child will only enter a woman who is *Tanamildjan* to it; in other words, the spirit child obeys the same laws, when choosing a mother, as a man does when choosing a wife.

Taboos Associated with the Living Willy-wagtail. The aborigines in southern, central and northern Australia regard the willy-wagtail with either fear or unfriendliness. Among the Adnyamatana tribe of the northern Flinders Ranges in South Australia[28] the willy-wagtail is looked upon as the harbinger of death; but along the northern coasts, the bird, although not actually feared, is much disliked because the aborigines consider that he is a liar and a mischievous tell-tale. Should the women learn any of the secrets of the men, even in small matters, the men believe that it is the willy-wagtail who told them. Because of his bad character in these matters, the men always hunt the willy-wagtail away before they discuss the secret matters of the tribe.

The Pitjandjara, like the Adnyamatana tribe, have a deep fear of the willy-wagtail. They will never kill it, nor even throw a stone at it. If anyone were so foolish as to do so, he would be inviting a catastrophe of no mean order, for the spirit of the willy-wagtail, becoming angry, would create huge storms of wind that would destroy everyone and everything. On the other hand, the willy-wagtail is looked upon as a useful guardian: if it calls at night, the aborigines know that enemies are approaching.

(*h*) *The Mythical Snake, Wanambi*

The Pitjandjara aborigines believe that a mythical snake, called wanambi, lives in the steep-sided rockhole, Uluru (Fig. 3), situated on the summit above the Tjukiki gorge.[29]

[28] Mountford, Field Notes, 1937.

[29] Previously, my informants, not being Ayers Rock men, therefore not fully conversant with either the topography or the myths, made a mistake in the identification of Uluru rockhole. (Mountford, 1948, p.102.)

Plate 104. The willy-wagtail woman, Tjinderi-tjinderiba: A, Boulders in cave, once infants of Tjinderi-tjinderiba, now source of aboriginal children; B, White line, once urine running from the camp of infants.

This wanambi, which is regarded as the most dangerous and unfriendly in the country, has its home in huge caverns under, not in, the waters of Uluru. The snake is many hundreds of yards long, has an enormous head, long projecting teeth and beard, and a skin which old Balinga said had the same colours as a rainbow, a form which the Ayers Rock wanambi sometimes assumes. If an aboriginal drinks at Uluru rockhole, or lights a fire near by, he will so offend the wanambi that it will rise in the air in the form of a rainbow, and kill the offender by biting his *kuran* (spirit) with its long teeth. As a still further punishment, the wanambi will take the water, not only from the Uluru rockhole, but from all the other springs and waterholes around the base of Ayers Rock.

When I visited Ayers Rock late in 1961, all the waterholes, with the exception of Mutitjilda (Fig. 3, and Pl. 19B) were dry, and Mutitjilda, which is considered one of the "safe" waters in this arid country, was almost exhausted. Munbun, a Pitjandjara man, my informant on that occasion, who had never seen Mutitjilda so low, was convinced that the wanambi at Uluru, probably angered by the behaviour of someone at his rockhole, was taking the water away from Ayers Rock as a punishment.

The Ayers Rock wanambi is so greatly feared that old Balinga would not let me go near the Uluru rockhole, although he pointed out its position to me (Fig. 3). Balinga was sure that, had I disobeyed him, the wanambi would have transformed himself into a rainbow, and killed us both.[30]

The myth of a huge snake that lives in waterholes (known to the anthropological world as the rainbow serpent), appears to belong, in one form or another, to all Australian tribes. There is little doubt that the bunyip was the same mythical creature.

The wanambi at Ayers Rock, and others in the Pitjandjara country, do not fall into the same category as the totemic beings of *tjukurapa* times for, although they, like the totemic beings, existed during the early days of the world, they did not create any part of the topography, nor did they change their form at the close of the creation period. The wanambi of *tjukurapa* times are the same as the wanambi of today.[31]

[30] The following personal experience will indicate the degree to which the aborigines look upon the wanambi as a living creature. During 1940, a number of aborigines took me to the Piltadi rockhole, on the eastern end of the Mann Ranges, the home of a particularly dangerous wanambi. My companions, afraid that since I was a stranger the wanambi might attack me, took me to the rockhole, and after "introducing" me, asked the wanambi not to harm me, because I was a friend of theirs. Needless to say, I suffered no harm. (Mountford, 1948, p.139.)

[31] Stanner (1961, pp.235-52), when discussing the myths associated with the rainbow serpent of the Murinbata tribe of the Daly river, refers to it as the "riteless myth". This statement is equally true about the rainbow serpent myth of the Pitjandjara aborigines. I have never seen, nor heard, of any ceremony associated with the wanambi myth.

Part Three

THE ART OF AYERS ROCK

The aborigines of central Australia employ the simplest art motifs of any living people; those used by the Pitjandjara in the decoration of their sacred objects, the kulpidji, *are particularly restricted.*

At Ayers Rock there are three distinct art forms:

(a) *The extinct art of the rock engravings, in which the motifs are very simple.*

(b) *The art of the sacred objects, the* kulpidji, *where both the form and number of engraved designs are heavily restricted by the prohibitions of the ritualistic life.*

(c) *The art of the caves, where the aborigines, free from ceremonial taboos and limited only by the motifs available in their own culture, are free to express themselves in any way they may desire.*

Chapter 8

THE ART OF THE ROCK ENGRAVINGS

A NUMBER of simple rock engravings were found at both Ayers Rock and Katatjuta. Several interesting aspects of this form of aboriginal art will be discussed before the designs illustrated in Figs. 4-7 are described.

(*a*) *Distribution*

Indentations, made up of a series of peck-marks or indentations in the rock surface (Mountford and Edwards, 1962B, Pl. 1), have a wide distribution in Australia. They extend from the Burra, a locality about 100 miles north of Adelaide in South Australia, to the northern and extreme north-western coasts of the continent; to the western districts of New South Wales and Queensland; and to widely separated localities in Tasmania. It is a curious fact, however, that this form of aboriginal art has not yet been found in the State of Victoria, or along the south-western or southern edges of the continent. In the writer's experience, too, rock engravings exist only near some form of water supply, such as rockholes, springs and temporary lagoons.

(*b*) *Origin*

There is little doubt that these pecked engravings are an ancient and extinct art. Whenever the author inquired about their origin from the tribalized natives of central Australia, he was told that they were not the work of any aboriginal, but of one or another of the totemic beings who created the world in *tjukurapa* (creation) times. In other words, the aborigines, not knowing the artists of the rock engravings, have given them mythical origin.

(*c*) *Age*

The rock engravings of north-eastern South Australia and central Australia, an area in which the writer has carried out considerable research, all show evidences of extreme age, such as extensive patination of surfaces of both the rock and the engravings; exfoliation of the engraved surface (Mountford and Edwards, 1963, p.142); and, at Yunta, earth movement that has taken place after a rock surface has been engraved (Mountford, 1929, Pl. 1, Fig. 4).

Basedow (1914, pp.195-210) was the first to draw attention to evidence that indicated the great antiquity of the rock engravings in South Australia. Some fifteen years later Mountford (1929, pp. 243-8) located and described an unusual rock engraving at Panaramitee north which bore a close resemblance to the head of a sea-going crocodile (*Crocodilus porosus*). In 1962 the author, in collaboration with R. Edwards, described and figured two additional marine creatures from the same area, a sea-going turtle and a salt-water fish (Mountford and Edwards, 1962, Article 174). The fact that the aborigines could not have pictured these creatures so accurately unless they had been conversant with their appearance suggests that a considerable time must have elapsed since these designs had been engraved. At present the nearest salt-water crocodile is a thousand miles north, and the nearest sea-coast over a hundred miles distant.

(*d*) *Motifs*

Although the designs of the rock engravings of Ayers Rock, Katatjuta and elsewhere in central Australia, (Mountford, 1960, Article 192) consist of simple forms (Figs 4-7), those in southern Australia are more varied and complex. Nevertheless, among the large number of designs recorded in South Australia (Mountford, 1929, pp.337-65; Mountford and Edwards, 1963, pp.131-46) and others, no one has, as yet, found a single representation of a human being or of a creature.[1] There are many engravings of reptiles, and a single incomplete example of an emu, lying on its side (Mountford and Edwards, 1963, Fig. 7B).

In western New South Wales, however, are numerous figures of animals, birds and human beings (McCarthy and Macintosh, 1962, pp.249-98). There are also several striking human figures, some wearing elaborate ceremonial head-dresses, at Koonawarra, western New South Wales (Mountford, 1962, pp.245-8) and at Eucola (unrecorded), on the Nullarbor plains of western South Australia.

(*e*) *Techniques*

At present we do not know, with any degree of certainty, how the pecked rock engravings were made. As it is possible, however, to make passably good imitations of these engravings by striking the rock surface with the sharp edge of a quartzite boulder held

[1] Since writing this, the writer has found engravings of human figures in the Red Gorge, Deception Creek, northern South Australia.

in the hand, it is reasonable to suppose that a similar tool would have been used to produce the rock engravings under discussion. These boulders, once discarded, would not be recognizable as tools.

The aborigines of central Australia still use a form of rock art that is somewhat related to the pecked rock engravings. In the arid parts of the continent the rocks are coated with a red-brown patina, which is destroyed when struck with a hard object, exposing the lighter coloured stone underneath. The aborigines have used this characteristic to produce their simple designs by pounding the rock surface with a small pebble (Mountford, 1955, pp.345-52).

Description of the Rock Engravings

Figure 4. This small, lightly engraved group was found on the sloping and vertical faces of Ayers Rock near the "body" of the willy-wagtail woman, Tjinderi-tjinderiba (Pl. 99A and Fig. 3). None of the engravings at this site have any obvious meaning, A being more complex than the remainder.

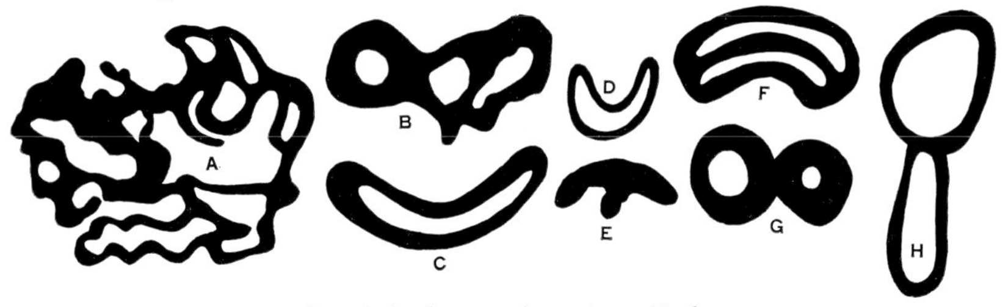

FIG. 4. Rock engravings, Ayers Rock.

Figure 5. These designs have been engraved on the flat surfaces around the Tiyin rockhole at the base of the most southerly dome of the Katatjuta group (Pl. 11B), the camping place of the mythical Liru snakes. A and D are snake-like designs; B, a series of circles; C, a concentric circle; and G, bird tracks. E and F are indecipherable.

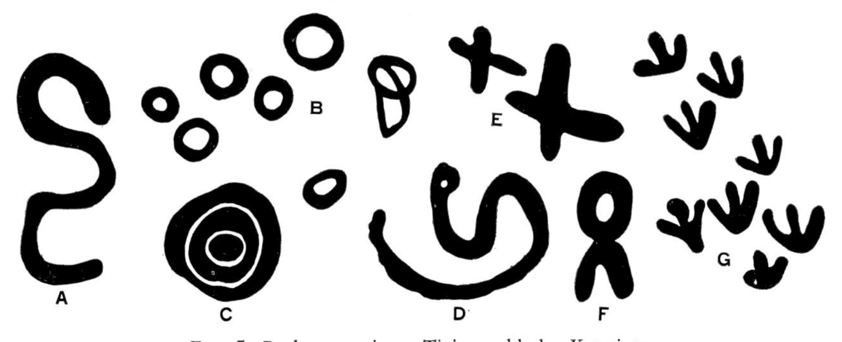

FIG. 5. Rock engravings, Tiyin rockhole, Katatjuta.

Figure 6. This text figure illustrates a number of engravings that have been cut into the rocks near the Wina rockhole in the valley of the mice women on the eastern side of Katatjuta (Mountford and Roberts, [n.d.], Map p.6). The majority of the engraved designs are either circles or linked circles. There are, however, barred circles at F, N, P, Q and S; concentric circles at K, L, M and S; a single bird track at R; and a number of bird and reptile tracks at O.

FIG. 6. Rock engravings, Wina rockhole, Katatjuta.

Figure 7. In the steep-sided Walpa (wind) gorge on the western side of the Katatjuta there are a number of small rockholes.

Many of the rock engravings on the northern side of the mouth of this gorge have already been recorded by Pringle and Kollosche (1958, pp.131-9). The majority of those illustrated in Fig. 7 are on the sloping rock surfaces around the Walpa rockhole (Mountford and Roberts, [n.d.], illustration p.8).

Engravings A and H are unusually complex abstract designs; F and L, concentric circles; M and C, barred circles; K and O, lines of bird tracks; J, an oval design enclosing a bird track, a common design at Panaramitee, South Australia (Mountford and Edwards, 1963, Fig. 3 G, K); L, a snake design; and G, probably a boomerang.

The rock engravings examined by the writer in other parts of central Australia, i.e. Korporilya, Iromba, Watelbring, Ngama and

Ewaninga (Mountford, 1960, Article 192), although sometimes in larger numbers, are almost as simple in design as those at Ayers Rock and Katatjuta.

Fig. 7. Rock engravings, Walpa Gorge, Katatjuta.

Rock engravings such as these are widely distributed, having been found in the U.S.A., Europe, the Sahara, South Africa and many other places. Some of the motifs are as simple as the majority illustrated in Figs 4-7, others are more complex.

It is possible that, in their simplest form, engravings of this type are examples of man's earliest attempt to portray his mental images in visual symbols. At first, these motifs would be simple, but as time went on the artist, by inventing new motifs and improving his techniques, would be able to express himself more fully.

Chapter 9

THE ART OF THE SACRED OBJECTS

THE *ḳulpidji* are the most sacred objects in the culture of the Pitjandjara tribe. The younger women and uninitiated youths do not even know of their existence, although it appears fairly certain that some of the older women would have heard about them. Nevertheless, no one who is not a fully initiated man is allowed to see or handle these *ḳulpidji* under pain of death.

Each *ḳulpidji* is looked upon as a concentrated mass of the life essence, *ḳurunba* (p.62), the aborigines believing that the mere physical contact of this sacred object with their body will cause the *ḳurunba* to flow into them, thus giving renewed strength and vitality (Mountford, 1948, p.146, illustration facing p.144).

The aborigines explained the related myths and the meanings of twenty *ḳulpidji* designs (Figs 8-25). These belong to five mythical stories: (*a*) the carpet-snakes, Kunia, and the venomous snakes, Liru; (*b*) the hare-wallabies, Mala, and the spirit dingo, Kulpunya; (*c*) the lizard, Kandju; (*d*) the marsupial moles, Itjari-tjari; and (*e*) the sleepy-lizard, Meta-lungana.

Description of the Sacred Objects

(*a*) *The Myth of the Carpet-snaḳes, Kunia, and the Venomous Snaḳes, Liru*

There are four *ḳulpidji* designs (Figs 8-11), belonging to this myth.

Figure 8. This *ḳulpidji* refers to the time when the carpet-snake men and women, Kunia, travelled from Maratjara to Ayers Rock,

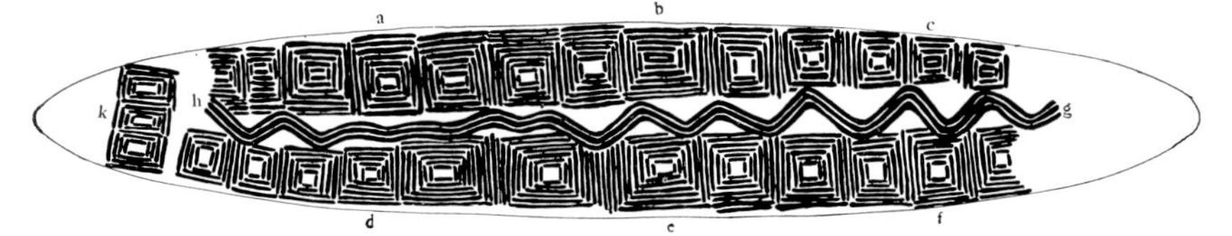

FIG. 8. Camps of carpet-snakes, Kunia, at Ayers Rock.

where they made their camp near the Uluru waterhole (Fig. 3).

The triple meandering line, g, h, refers to the track made by the carpet-snake people as they travelled to Ayers Rock, and the series of concentric squares, a, b, c, d, e, f and k, to their camping places.

At the close of the creation period, the tracks of the carpet-snakes were transformed into deep gutters on the southern face of Ayers Rock (Pl. 7A), and their camps into many circular rockholes (similar to Pl. 72A) on the summit.

Figure 9. The engravings on this sacred object refer to the time when the Kunia (carpet-snake) women at Ayers Rock collected food for themselves and their families.

The many concentric circles, a, b, c, d, etc., on the face of this *ḳulpidji* represent the breasts of the carpet-snake women; the groups of triple parallel lines, their body scars; and the lines of dots, the wild figs the women had gathered.

The women were changed into large boulders in the Tjukiki gorge (Pl. 10A, B, and Fig. 3), and the fruit into the fig-trees, *jili*, which grow among those boulders.

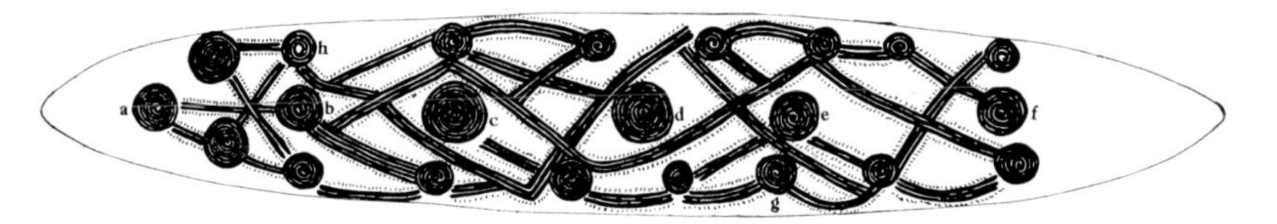

Fig. 9. Carpet-snakes, Kunia women, at Ayers Rock.

Figure 10. The engraved designs symbolize a party of mythical venomous snakes, the Liru, who, travelling from the west, made their camp on the southern dome of Katatjuta (Pl. 11B).

The meandering lines, a, b, c, d, e, etc., indicate the tracks made by the venomous snake men, and the groups of concentric circles, n, n, o, o, etc., the decorations which the men had painted on their bodies. These decorations were similar to those shown on the figure to the right.

Fig. 10. Venomous snake-men, Liru, travelling to Katatjuta (Mt Olga).

Figure 11. The designs in Fig. 11 refer to the time when the young Liru men, camping at Katatjuta, were preparing to attack the carpet-snake people at Ayers Rock.

The concentric circles, c, c, etc., symbolize the painted body decorations on the bodies of the young Liru men (see Fig. 10); the groups of curving triple lines, d, d, etc., the marks made in the sand as the young snakes wandered from place to place; and the crescentic designs, m, m, etc., their camping places. These camps have since been transformed into a group of rocky domes to the south of Katatjuta (Pl. 12A).

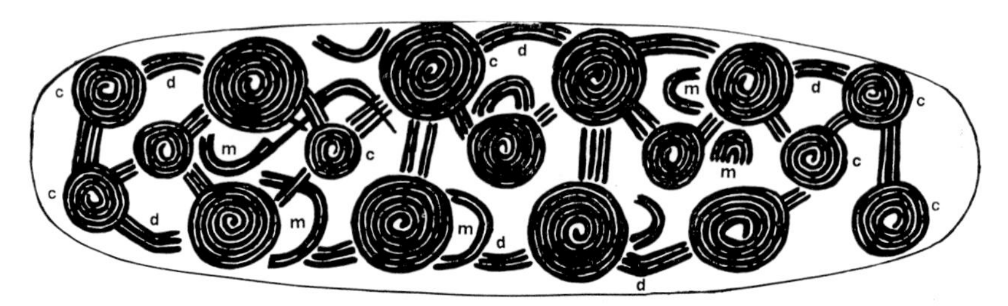

Fig. 11. Venomous snake-men, Liru, at Katatjuta (Mt Olga).

(*b*) *The Myth of the Hare-wallabies, Mala, and the Spirit Dingo, Kulpunya*

Eleven *kulpidji* designs (Figs 12-21) belong to this extensive myth. Although, undoubtedly, there would have been a *kulpidji* belonging to the kingfisher-woman, Lunba, the aborigines did not have one in their collection.

Figure 12. The designs on this *kulpidji* illustrate a number of old Mala men asleep in their camps on the northern side of Ayers Rock.

The groups of concentric circles, a, b, c, d, etc., symbolize the sleeping men, and the groups of triple parallel lines, g, h, j, k, the scars on their chests.

The bodies of the old Mala tribesmen are now large boulders

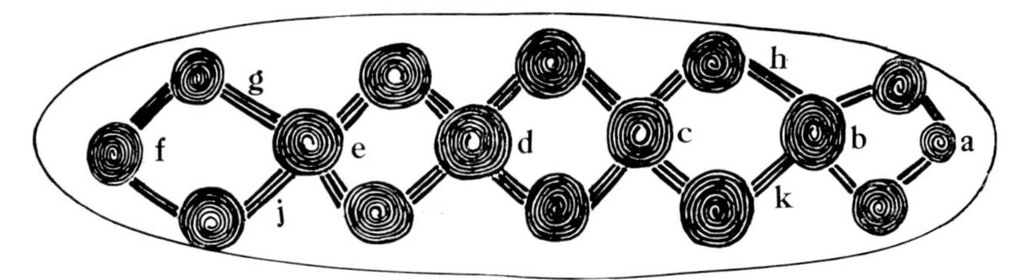

Fig. 12. Old Mala men asleep in their camps.

piled up against the side of Ayers Rock (Pl. 49A) adjacent to the Tjinindi rockhole (Pl. 98B and Fig. 3).

Figure 13. The engravings on this *ḳulpidji* illustrate a number of old Mala tribesmen decorating themselves to take part in the initiation rituals of their youths.

The concentric circles, a, a, b, b, etc., symbolize a number of Mala men decorating themselves, and the groups of connecting lines, the painted designs on their bodies. The initiates (represented by the groups of concentric circles, c) are asleep behind their windbreak at d.

The old men are now isolated boulders (Pls 60A, 61A) near the initiation cave of the Mala men (Fig. 3) and the sleeping youths, smaller boulders near by (Pl. 60B).

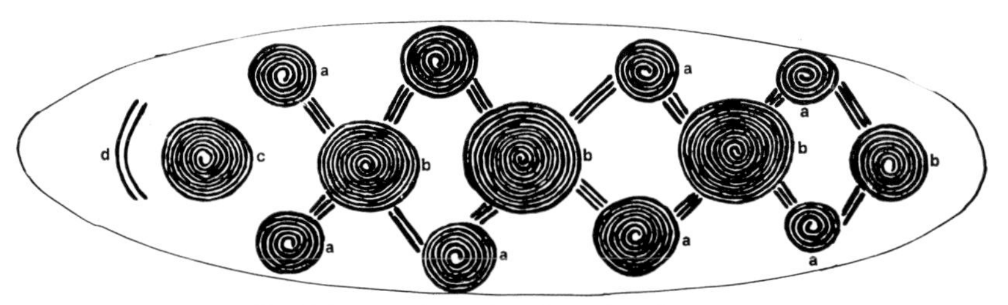

Fig. 13. Mala men decorating themselves for ceremony.

Figure 14. The *ḳulpidji* illustrated in Fig. 14 refers to a number of old Mala men chanting the songs and performing the ceremonies of initiation while the young men are lying face-downward on the ground beside them. At a given stage, the lads are allowed to sit up and watch the rituals while the old men explained their meanings.

The concentric circles a, a, b, b, etc., on the face of the *ḳulpidji* symbolize the old men taking part in the rituals; the groups of straight lines, their body decorations; and the crescentic designs, c, c, c, etc., on the edge of the *ḳulpidji*, the initiates lying on the ground.

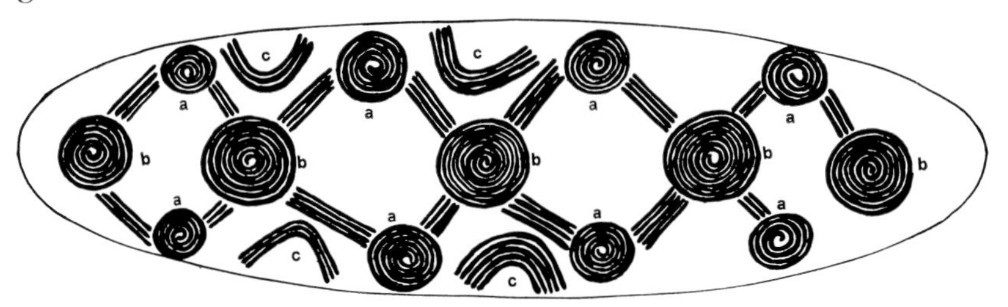

Fig. 14. Mala men and initiates at ceremony.

Figure 15. These engraved designs refer to the *naldawata* pole (Pl. 54A), which was once erected by the Mala tribesmen in the middle of their ceremonial initiation ground.

The central line of barred rectangles, a, b, c, d, e, symbolizes the decorated *naldawata* pole with a feathered cross-piece, f, from which many *kulpidji* are suspended (shown as groups of crescents, g, h, i, j, k, and n). The concentric circles, m, m, o, o, p, p, r, r, s, s and t, as well as the intersecting groups of barred rectangles, a, b, c, etc., symbolize the coloured circular designs of eagle-down fastened with blood to the *naldawata* pole.

The *naldawata* pole, with the cross-piece that supports the many *kulpidji*, has since been transformed into an immense slab of rock on the north-westerly corner of Ayers Rock (Pl. 54A and Fig. 3).

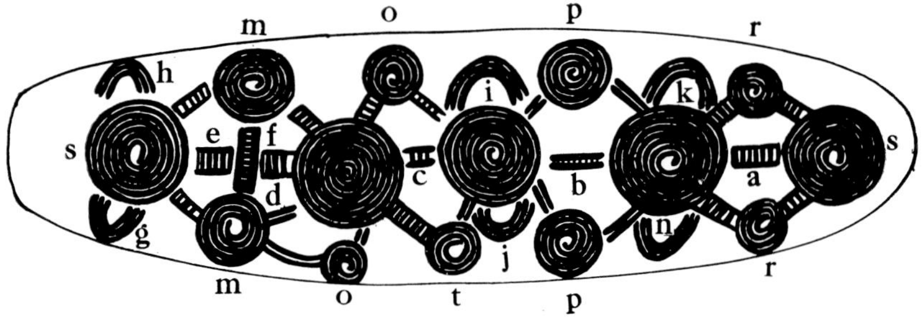

FIG. 15. Naldawata pole at Mala initiation ceremony.

Figure 16. This *kulpidji* belongs to Tabudja (Pl. 37B and Fig. 3), a low rocky hill on the north-eastern corner of Ayers Rock, where the mythical Mala women gathered and cooked the yellow-fruited solanum, *yirtumba*, as food for themselves and their families.

The series of dots in Fig. 16 symbolize the lines of fruit which the Mala women had laid out on the ground, and the groups of parallel lines throughout the design the ashes of the fire in which the women cooked their food.

The lines of *yirtumba* fruit are now low reefs of stone at Tabudja (Pl. 38A), and the cooked food, mounds of stone (Pl. 37A). Although the ashes of the cooking fires would almost certainly have been transformed into some natural feature, my informants did not point them out.

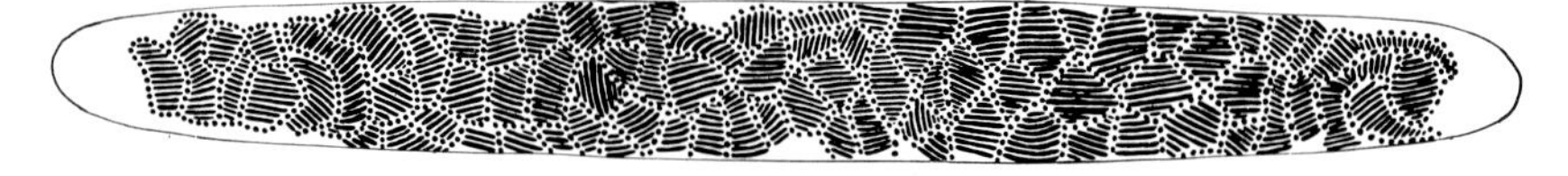

FIG. 16. Mala women at Tabudja.

Figure 17. This *kulpidji* refers to an old Mala tribesman who once made a camp so that he could prevent the women from leaving Tabudja and spying on the initiation rituals of the men.

The concentric circles, b, c, d, symbolize the camps of the old Mala man, and the groups of crescents, a, a, a, a, his body scars.

The camps are now a series of caves on the northern side of Ayers Rock not far from Tabudja (Pl. 45A, B, and Fig. 3); the old Mala tribesman, a long column of stone (Pl. 46B); and the places where he and his companions performed ceremonies to pass away the time, small circular caves high up on the side of the Rock (Pl. 44A).

FIG. 17. Old Mala man guarding women at Tabudja.

Figure 18. These engraved designs belong to the camp of the Mala women and children on the north-eastern corner of Ayers Rock (Fig. 3). The concentric circles, a, b, c, indicate the three camps of the Mala women; the groups of crescentic designs, d, d, d, etc., places where the women had defecated; and the meandering lines, e, e, etc., the wandering tracks made by the venomous snake-man, Liru, who raped one of the women (Pl. 31A, B, Fig. 19).

The camps of the Mala women and children have since been transformed into a long cave (Pl. 33A), which the aborigines divide into three sections (Pls 33B, 34A, B); the excreta of the women into groups of boulders outside of the same caves and the track of the snake-man, Liru, into a dark water-stain on the floor of a spectacular gorge near by (Pl. 32A).

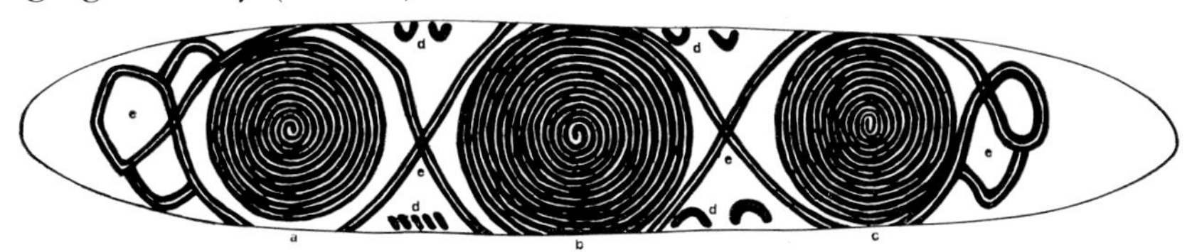

FIG. 18. Mala women and children in their camp.

Figure 19. After the venomous snake-men, Liru, had destroyed the harmless carpet-snakes, Kunia, on the south side of Ayers Rock, a young Liru man, anxious to cause more trouble, travelled to the camp of the Mala women on the northern side of Ayers Rock, where he caught and raped one of them. The design of this *kulpidji*, which is duplicated on either end, illustrates the incident. The body of the Liru man is represented by the concentric circles, a, a; his legs by the groups of parallel lines, e, e, e, e; and his arms by similar designs at f, f, f, f.

The concentric circles, c, c, indicate the body of the Mala woman; the groups of lines, k, k, k, k, her legs; and g, g, g, g, her arms. The concentric circles, b, b, etc., on either edge of the *kulpidji*, symbolize the knee marks which the Liru youth made in the sand as he copulated with the Mala woman. These knee marks are now a series of pot-holes on a level pavement (Pl. 31A) on the north-westerly corner of Ayers Rock.

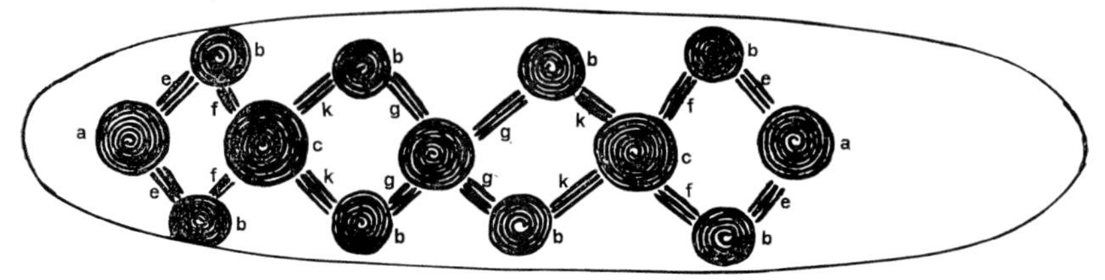

FIG. 19. The Liru man and Mala woman.

Figure 20. A spirit dingo, Kulpunya, was created by the Windulka (mulga-seed) men of Kikingura to punish and destroy the Mala people of Ayers Rock. The engraved designs on these *kulpidji* (Fig. 20A, B) symbolize, in a particularly simple form, the body of that mythical creature.

The concentric circles, a, on Fig. 20A, indicate the head of Kulpunya; crescent b and c, his ribs; the two crescents at d, his collar bone; and the three at e, his body scars.

Other bodily features are indicated on Fig. 20B. The concentric circles, a, symbolize Kulpunya's navel; line b, his penis; c, his windpipe; d, e, his ears; g and f, his back legs; h, k, his front legs; and the double crescent n, o, Kulpunya seated on the ground.

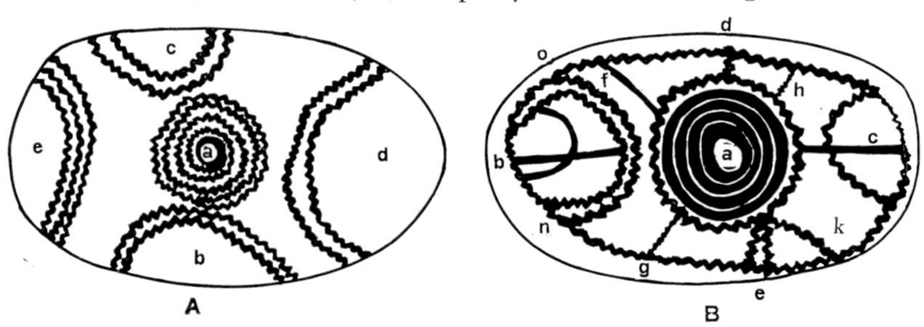

FIG. 20. Body of the spirit dingo, Kulpunya.

Figure 21. This *kulpidji* also deals with the spirit dingo, Kulpunya. The crescents at a represent the windbreak of Kulpunya's camp (unlocalized), and b, b, c, c, e, e, and f, his tracks in the sand as he crept along the base of Ayers Rock. These tracks are now low bushes and boulders on the plain, and the crescents, d, d, and g, g, etc., places along the northern face of Ayers Rock, where Kulpunya paused (probably Pls 67B, 68A, 69A, B, and 70B). According to the myth, the line h was once a fallen tree over which Kulpunya stepped. This tree is now a long boulder (Pl. 70B) near the Tjinindi rockhole (Fig. 3).

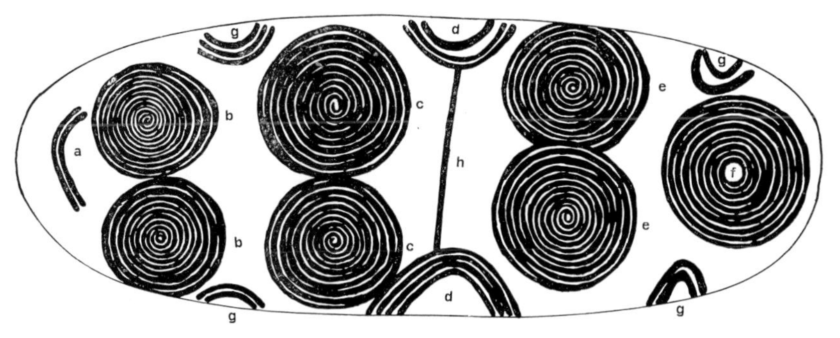

FIG. 21. Journey of spirit dingo, Kulpunya.

Figure 22. When Kulpunya first reached Ayers Rock, the Mala women were asleep in their camp (Pls 33, 34). At the time the spirit dingo was attacking and killing the eagle-chick, Kudrun, the Mala women endeavoured to escape, but without success.

The parallel lines on the *kulpidji*, arranged in the form of concentric squares, symbolize the footprints of the terrified women, and the holes drilled in the surface, their toe-marks in the sand. The concentric squares represent the camps of the women.

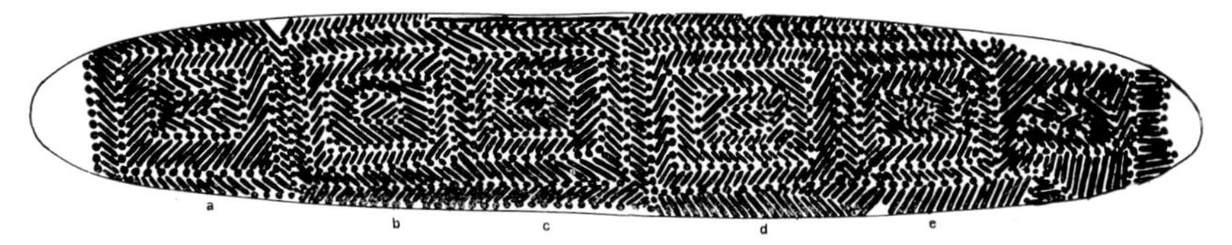

FIG. 22. Kulpunya and the Mala women.

(*c*) *The Myth of the Lizard, Kandju*

The myth of the lizard, Kandju, who lost his boomerang in the soft sand of Uluru (Ayers Rock), and his subsequent search is illustrated on this *kulpidji* (see p.114).

Figure 23. The meandering lines, such as e, e, indicate the gutters which Kandju made in the sand as he searched for his missing weapon; the smaller concentric circles, a, a, etc., his knee marks as he crawled from place to place in his search; the short parallel lines, b, b, etc., gutters and pot-holes on the side of Ayers Rock where he had dug for the missing weapon; and the dots at c, c, trees on the nearby open plain. The three large groups of concentric circles, f, f, f, represent waterholes where Kandju either camped or had a drink; and the pair of curved lines, d, on the left, the missing boomerang.

The gutters which Kandju made in the sand are now deep clefts in the western side of Ayers Rock; his knee marks, large pot-holes (Pls 73A, 74A); the waterholes, now Kandju soak (Pl. 73B); and the boomerang, the curving edge of a large pot-hole on the side of the Rock (Pl. 77A).

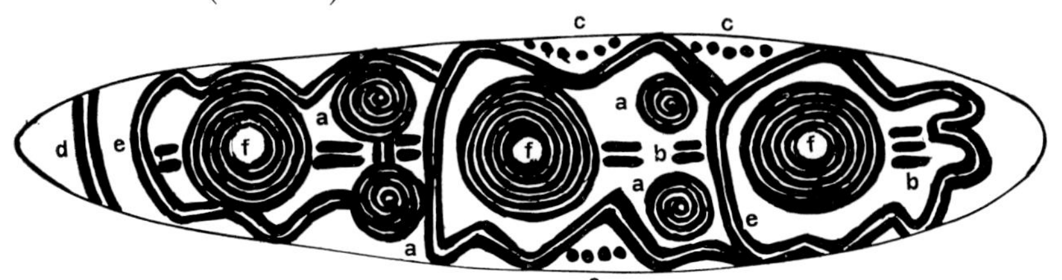

FIG. 23. The lizard, Kandju, and his lost boomerang.

(*d*) *The Myth of the Marsupial Mole, Itjari-tjari*

The totemic place of the marsupial mole, Itjari-tjari, is on the western side of Ayers Rock (Fig. 3).

Figure 24. The concentric circles, a, refer to the wet-weather shelters of the marsupial moles; c, to a dry-weather camp; and d, the groups of curving lines at either end of the *kulpidji*, to the windbreak of the dry-weather camp. The concentric circles, b, illustrate an inaccessible rockhole called Kadu, and the groups of curved lines, e, e, etc., the arms of the marsupial moles as they scratched holes in the ground in their search for food.

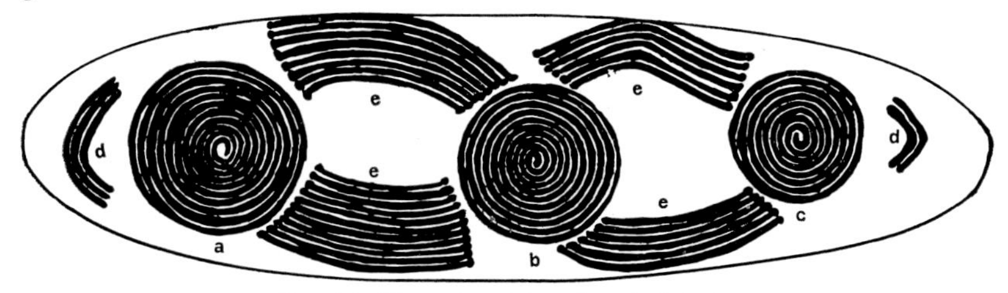

FIG. 24. The marsupial mole, Itjari-tjari.

The wet-weather shelters, a, are now attractive caves at ground level (Pls 85A, 87A); the dry-weather camp, b, an immense bowl high up the Rock (Pl. 86B); the windbreak, d, d, the high precipice that surrounds it (Pl. 86A, B); and the holes which the marsupial moles once scratched in the sand, deep pot-holes on the steep sides of Ayers Rock (Pl. 85A).

(*e*) *The Myth of the Sleepy-lizard Man, Meta-lungana*

The sleepy-lizard man, Meta-lungana, whose totemic places are on the southern side of Ayers Rock, was burned to death because he was too mean to share the emus he had caught with his neighbours, the carpet-snake people.

Figure 25A, B. The camp fire where Meta-lungana cooked the emus is represented by the group of concentric circles, d, d, etc., on Fig. 25A, and the emus he had captured by the designs, g, g, etc., on Figs 25A and B.

Sometimes the sleepy-lizard man would dismember the birds with his stone knife, so that his neighbours would not see the meat, and carry it to his wet-weather camp (crescents a, in Fig. 25A). The portions of the dismembered emu are indicated by the triple lines joining the concentric circles in Fig. 25A, and the legs by concentric circles, d, d, etc., in Fig. 25B.

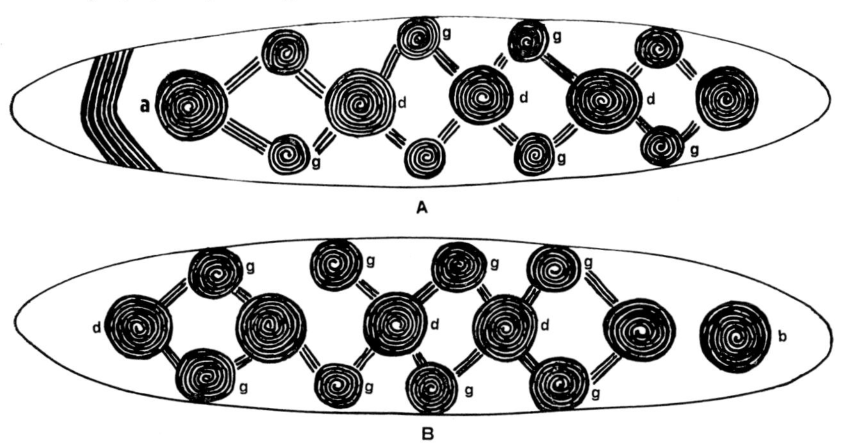

FIG. 25. The sleepy-lizard, Meta-lungana, and the emu meat.

The cooking place is now a rockhole, Kalaia-tjunda, which means emu leg (Pl. 92B and Fig. 3); portions of the dismembered emu, either columns of rock (Pls 92A, 97A), shallow caves on the side of the Rock (Pl. 93A), or split boulders (Pl. 95A, B). The wet-weather camp of the sleepy-lizard man is now a long cave near the south-western corner of the Rock (Pl. 94A).

Analysis of Designs engraved on Kulpidji

An analysis of the *kulpidji* illustrated in Figs 8-25 shows that the art forms engraved on their surfaces are much more limited than those painted in the caves of Ayers Rock.

In order to show the limited number of motifs employed and the wide range of meanings associated with each one, it has been decided to analyse them under three headings: (*a*) The motifs employed; (*b*) the number of times each motif is used; (*c*) The different meanings associated with each motif.

(*a*) *The Motifs Employed*

Eight motifs, shown diagrammatically in Fig. 26 have been engraved on the Ayers Rock *kulpidji*. They are:

Figure 26A. Concentric circles, a common motif in the art of central Australia, which usually starts as a spiral and finishes as a series of circles.

Figure 26B. Triple parallel lines, often used to link the design elements of the *kulpidji*.

Figure 26C. A single straight line, seldom used.

Figure 26D. An unusual motif which appears to be limited to the Pitjandjara tribe. Mountford (1962, Figs 3A, B, E, F, G, H) records similar designs on *kulpidji* associated with the mulga-seed people of Kikingura, in the western Petermann Ranges. This motif is used on only two of the Ayers Rock *kulpidji*, once as a random pattern (Fig. 16), and once as a series of concentric squares (Fig. 22).

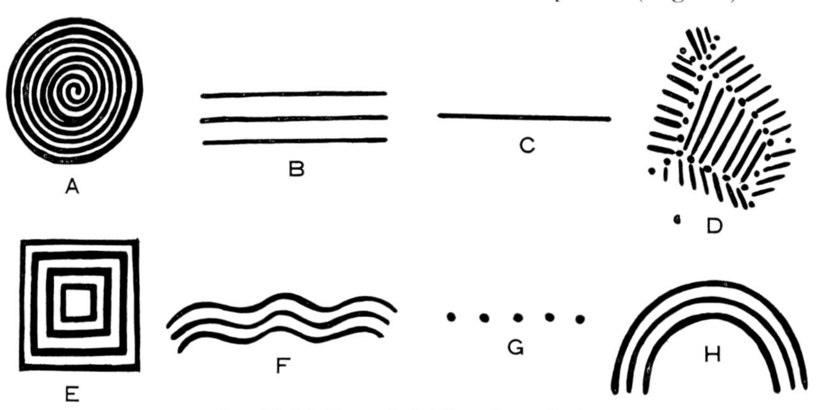

FIG. 26. Motifs on *kulpidji* at Ayers Rock.

Figure 26E. A series of concentric squares, a modification of the concentric circles. Although this motif is not used by the Aranda tribesmen to the east, its use extends west and north-west from Ayers Rock for almost a thousand miles until, by the time it has reached the coast, it is largely replaced by the interlocking key pattern (Davidson, 1937, Fig. 67).

Figure 26F. Triple meandering lines, seldom used on the Ayers Rock *kulpidji*.

Figure 26G. A series of dots, which, apart from those in designs such as Fig. 16, are seldom used.

Figure 26H. Triple crescentic lines, a common motif on the Ayers Rock *kulpidji* and in the sacred art of central Australia.

(*b*) *The Number of Occasions when a Specific Motif was Used*

Concentric circles (Fig. 26A), 14 times; triple parallel lines (Fig. 26B), 8 times; single straight line (Fig. 26C), twice; dots and straight lines (Fig. 26D), twice; concentric squares (Fig. 26E), once; triple meandering lines (Fig. 26F), four times; lines of dots (Fig. 26G), 3 times; and triple crescents (Fig. 26H), eleven times.

This list shows that the three most commonly used motifs, i.e. concentric circles, parallel straight lines and crescents, make up 73 per cent of the total designs.

(*c*) *The Different Meanings Attached to Each Motif*

Concentric circles (Fig. 26A), breasts of women; body decorations; designs on the *naldawata* pole; man lying down asleep; men dancing, or the place where the men danced; camps and waterholes; knee-marks in sand and the head and navel of the spirit dingo, Kulpunya.

Triple parallel straight lines (Fig. 26B), scars on the bodies of men; body decorations; ceremonial *naldawata* pole and its decorations; legs and arms of men and women and lines of emu meat.

Single straight lines (Fig. 26C), bodily features of mythical dog, Kulpunya, and the trunk of a tree.

Dots and straight lines (Fig. 26D), footmarks and toe-prints of women; lines of fruit and ashes of camp fire.

Concentric squares (Fig. 26E), camps.

Triple meandering lines (Fig. 26F), tracks of snakes and lizards.

Lines of dots (Fig. 26G), lines of fruit and trees on plain.

Triple crescents (Fig. 26H), camps with windbreak; men lying on the ground; decorations on *naldawata* pole; places where women had defecated; bodily features of mythical dingo, and a boomerang.

Summary

This analysis has shown that the motifs available to the Pitjandjara tribesmen for illustrating the myths on the sacred *kulpidji* are exceedingly limited, consisting of only eight designs of which three form 73 per cent of the total used.

Under these conditions, it is inevitable that each design would have a number of different meanings associated with it. Yet, in spite of this, there is a certain resemblance between these designs and the subjects they represent.

For instance, the concentric circles represent breasts of women, camps and waterholes, tracks of dingoes, knee marks in sand, and so on. Similarly, parallel straight lines refer to paths, body scars and legs and arms of aborigines; triple crescentic designs to the windbreak of a camp, men lying on the ground or a boomerang; and triple meandering lines to the tracks of snakes and lizards.

It is evident, however, that only the tribesmen who knew both the myth and the particular *kulpidji* intimately would be able to explain their meanings to the investigator.

Another characteristic, mentioned earlier, is the limited symbolism employed in the sacred art of the *kulpidji* when compared with the much wider range in the secular art of the cave paintings.

This is undoubtedly due to the fact that the artist decorating the *kulpidji* is heavily restricted by the age-old customs and taboos of the ceremonial ground, where everything must remain unaltered from age to age (p.23).

On the other hand, the secular artist, being comparatively unrestricted by ceremonial taboos, and freer to develop his own ideas, is able to use a much wider range of designs in his art.

Associated with each *kulpidji* are a number of chants, which commemorate the exploits of the mythical hero with whom the sacred object is associated. Unfortunately the failure of the equipment prevented the recording of all but a few of these chants.

Chapter 10

THE ART OF THE CAVE PAINTINGS

Introduction

THE paintings in the caves of Ayers Rock are not as colourful as the x-ray art of western Arnhem Land, nor have they the strong feeling of movement so evident in the Mimi art of the same area.[1]

Neither do they belong to the secret life of the aborigines in the same manner as those associated with the Walbiri myth of the snake, Yarapi, at Ngama, nor the designs in the cave of the mythical emu at Lukiri. In both the Ngama and Lukiri caves the paintings are so sacred that no aboriginal is allowed to see them until he is approaching middle age.[2]

There is no doubt that the paintings at Ayers Rock belong to the secular side of aboriginal life. Most of the caves that provide the aborigines with good shelter are decorated with paintings, the back wall of some of them (for example, Sites 2 and 6) being entirely covered with a mosaic of designs, painted heterogeneously one over the other (Figs 30 and 35).

Although many of the paintings in the initiation cave (Site 9), may refer to myths unknown to the women, there is no evidence to show that the paintings themselves are part of the ceremonial life.

Rate of Change of Cave Paintings

By a fortunate circumstance, the writer is able to show that when the aborigines were living permanently at Ayers Rock there was a comparatively rapid change in the designs on the walls of the Mutitjilda cave (Site 2). An examination of Fig. 30, which is a complete record of the designs in this cave in 1940, and the overlay (Fig. 30A) taken from a photograph by Michael Terry made in 1930 (Pl. 105) show that a number of paintings visible on the earlier date had been entirely obliterated and replaced by others ten years

[1] Mountford, 1956, pp.112-83.
[2] Mountford, Field Notes, 1959, 1960.

later. It is reasonable to expect that similar changes would have taken place at the other cave painting sites at Ayers Rock.

Age of Paintings

It is to be expected that the present-day paintings at Ayers Rock will not have a long life. The paintings at Mutitjilda (Site 2) and those in the initiation cave (Site 9), first investigated by the author in 1940, when compared with the same paintings twenty years later show that during that time many have become much fainter and some have disappeared.

There is little doubt that, unless special precautions are taken to preserve them, there will be few examples of aboriginal art to be seen in the caves of Ayers Rock after a few decades.

Methods of Recording Cave Paintings

Two methods of recording were used. During 1940 the author and his companion, the late Mr L. E. Sheard, completed a scale drawing of the Mutitjilda cave (Fig. 30, Site 2) with colour notes, a task which occupied a number of days. Since time was limited on most other occasions, the author photographed the paintings in detail, usually with colour film. By including a six-inch scale in each photograph, it was possible to build up an excellent mosaic from which the text figures were traced.

All the recognizable cave paintings in the twelve main sites (Fig. 27) at Ayers Rock have been recorded in Figs 28-43. There are, however, a number of incomplete and faded groups among the isolated boulders and shallow caves, particularly along the northern face of Ayers Rock, which would be worth investigating and recording.

Significance of the Cave Paintings

An examination of the cave paintings reveals the fact that most of the designs are so abstract as to render any definite opinions about their meanings valueless without the explanation of the artist who produced them. Nevertheless, it is possible, on occasions, to arrive at an approximate meaning of a cave painting by comparing it with similar designs which have previously been made and interpreted by the Pitjandjara aborigines themselves.[3]

In general, my informants could not understand the meanings of the paintings in the caves at Ayers Rock, although occasionally one of them would see a design which had been explained to him by some old man.

[3] The author has collected approximately five hundred sheets of crayon drawings, mostly the work of Pitjandjara men. The majority of the many thousands of designs on these sheets of brown paper have been interpreted by the artists who produced them.

Techniques of Cave Painting

The techniques of painting the designs on the walls of the caves at Ayers Rock are simple. The pigments are red and yellow ochres, white pipe-clay and powdered charcoal. These pigments, after being ground to a creamy-like consistency on a rough stone, are applied to the painting surface with either the forefinger or a brush made from a strip of bark chewed at one end.[4]

Description of Cave Paintings and their Sites

There are twelve major cave painting sites around the base of Ayers Rock. These are indicated in Fig. 27.

Site 1

This is a large oval cave high up the southern side of Ayers Rock (Pl. 23A) which, according to the myth, was once the open mouth of the carpet-snake woman, Kunia Ingridi, mourning over the death of her son. As she did so, the angry and distressed mother spat out such large quantities of *arukwita*, the spirit of disease and death, that it impregnated the cave and the ground at its base for some distance on either side (see dotted line, Fig. 3). The aborigines

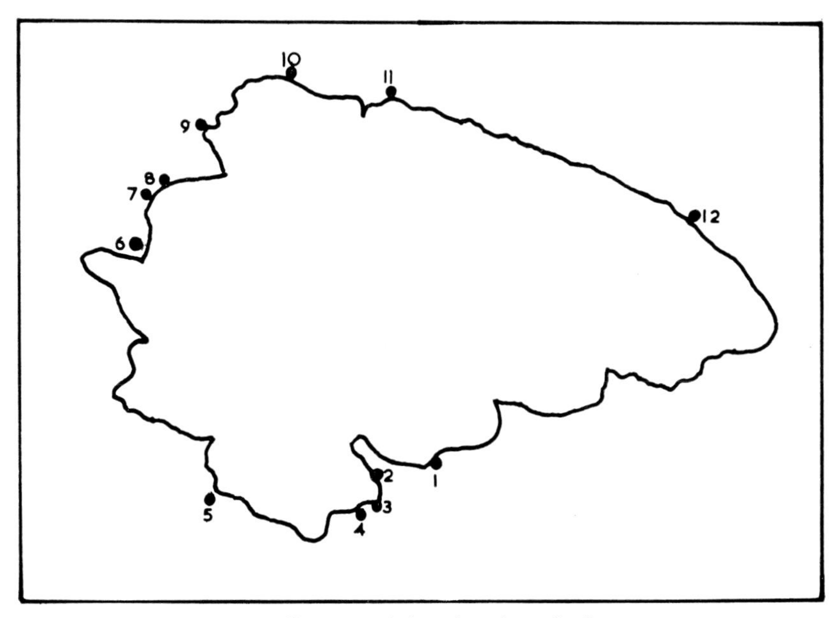

FIG. 27. Cave painting sites, Ayers Rock.

[4] Mountford (1937, p.434, plate facing p.436) describes and illustrates the techniques used by the desert aborigines in painting the designs on the cave walls.

believe that, if they approach closer than two hundred yards to this dreaded area, the *arukwita* will kill them.

Nevertheless, high up in the back of the cave (Pl. 23A), I located a number of faded paintings, some of which were unlike those elsewhere in the caves of Ayers Rock. The discovery of these examples of aboriginal art indicates that the cave was not always under a taboo, as at present.

Figure 28. There are four large bird tracks (Fig. 28A, B, C, D) on the left hand of Site 1, one of them being over four feet long. To the right, at F, there is a "tree-like" figure[5] in red, over-lying an incomplete complex painting in white, which bears some resemblance to Fig. 35N, in the cave of the marsupial mole (Site 6). G is another

FIG. 28. Cave paintings, Site 1.

"tree" design. Group H is made up of two "tree" designs and a particularly complex figure that bears more than a passing resemblance to a crayon drawing (Mountford, 1937, Fig. 11) depicting an Aranda sacred object of the honey-ant totem of Alabina, near Mt Zeil.

Figure 29. A, F, are two unusual cave paintings the meanings of which are not evident; B, G, two "tree" symbols; C, an unusual design of unknown meaning; and D, a series of circles. On the left, at E, there are many human, animal and bird tracks.

Site 2

This site, Mutitjilda cave, is a shelter about thirty feet long on the western wall of the Mutitjilda gorge (Pl. 18A, Fig. 3), immediately

[5] This is a comparatively common motif in the caves of Ayers Rock. As a similar motif on a crayon drawing (Mountford, 1938, Fig. 2) represents a mulga-tree, this motif, for the sake of convenience, will be referred to in the descriptions as the "tree" design, though I am well aware that this may not always be the true interpretation.

Cave paintings, Mutitjilda Gorge

below the severed nose of Kulikudjeri, the leader of the venomous Liru snakes (Pl. 21A).

I first visited this cave in 1935, and again in 1940, when, as mentioned earlier, the late Mr L. E. Sheard and I made a complete scale drawing of the paintings (Fig. 30).

Photo Michael Terry

PLATE 105. Paintings in Mutitjilda Cave, 1935.

A comparison of the paintings on the left-hand side of Site 2, photographed by Michael Terry in 1930 (pl. 105), and those recorded by Mr Sheard and me in 1940 (Fig. 30), shows that during the intervening ten years, when the aborigines were still following their tribal life at Ayers Rock, there had been a comparatively rapid change in the paintings on the walls of the Mutitjilda cave.

Fig. 30 (with the overlay in place) illustrates the paintings on the left-hand wall of Mutitjilda, when, in 1930, Michael Terry took the photograph; the designs on Fig. 30 (without the overlay), the paintings which my companion and I recorded in 1940.

The designs, A, B, C, D, E, F, G, H and K, shown in full lines (see overlay) have in a space of ten years been practically obliterated and replaced by other designs, such as A, B, H, etc. (Fig. 30). The position of the tail of the snake, too (L, Fig. 30), has been changed.

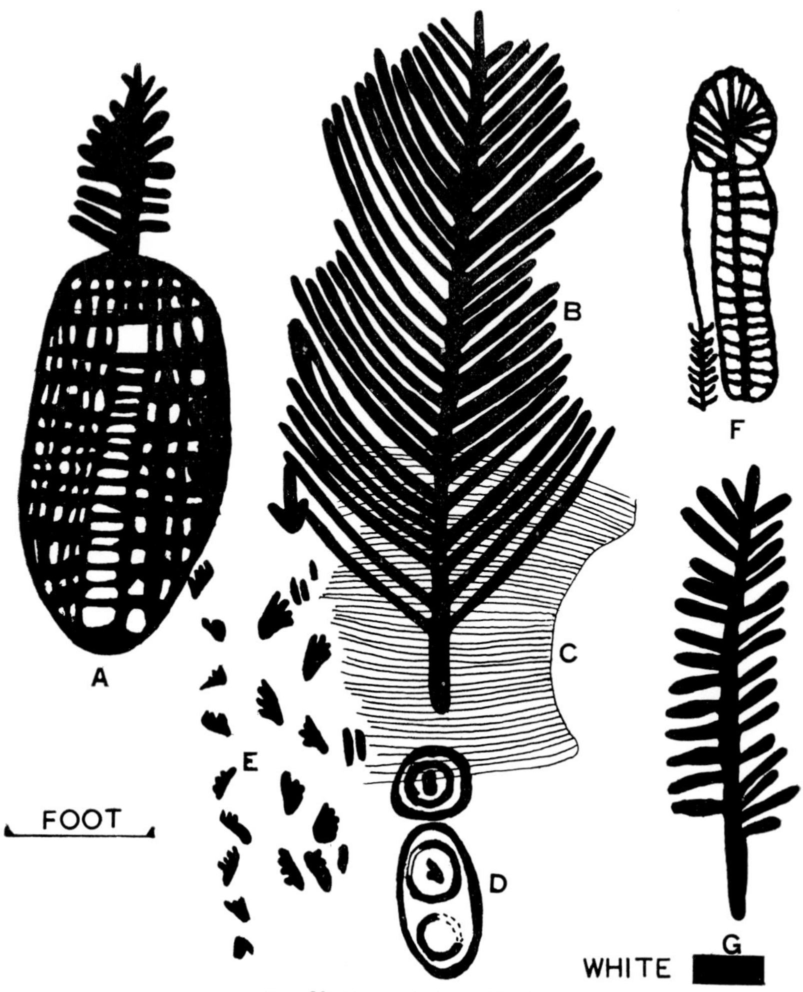

FIG. 29. Cave paintings, Site 1.

Figure 30. There is a dingo at A, and a curious anchor-like design at B. A number of simple representations of the human figure are scattered on the wall of the cave; groups at J, T and N; single figures at O, R, S, U, and other places; and another above M, wearing a tall elaborate head-dress.

At D, E, and F, on the upper edge of the frieze, are the remnants of large human figures with upstretched arms similar to those at V, on the lower right, and in particular to those in Fig. 36K and M in the initiation cave (Site 9). When these were first painted, they must have occupied a considerable space on the cave wall. Later artists have, however, overpainted and almost obliterated these large and, without doubt, in their day, striking designs.

Paintings P and W are "maps" similar to those used by the desert aborigines to depict the travel routes of one or another of the mythical heroes. The multiple parallel lines connecting the circles symbolize the route they followed, and the circles their camping places. Mountford (1938, p.246, Fig. 5) records similar designs describing the journeys of a mythical man, Wati Jula.

There is a "tree" design between E and F; curious grid-like patterns between D and E; and groups of concentric circles at Q. One long line of dingo tracks starting from the floor of the cave at M extends vertically for several feet and another, which crosses the "map" design W. There are many paintings scattered throughout the whole frieze the meanings of which are unknown.

FIG. 31. Cave paintings, Site 3.

Site 3

This site is a shallow cave about eleven feet long facing the open plain, only a few yards south of Mutitjilda rock shelter (Site 2).

When I first visited this cave in 1935, the paintings were clear and fresh-looking. At the present time, owing to their exposed position and the effects of the elements, many of the designs have practically disappeared.

Figure 31. The central and still the most easily distinguished figure is the dingo, K, which one of my informants tentatively identified as Kulpunya, the spirit dingo, who attacked and destroyed the Mala people on the northern side of Ayers Rock. N is a human figure with radiating lines from his head and penis. There are also simple human figures at A, B and G; tracks of birds and creatures at D, E, J, M and O; the single footprint of a human being at D; and a snake and shield-like design at C. There is no reasonable explanation for paintings F, H, L, and those which are adjacent to the bird tracks at O.

In 1935 I found two paintings on the rocks high above Site 3. Fig. 43H is an excellent representation of an emu; and Fig. 43G, a particularly complex circular design. These have now disappeared.

Site 4

There is a pile of huge boulders on the plain at the base of Ayers Rock immediately under the cliff (Pl. 20B). Under these boulders, on a curving face about thirty-five feet long, there is a colourful line of human figures, reptiles and abstract designs. These paintings, in particular those on the right-hand side of the panel, being totally protected from the elements, have suffered little damage (Fig. 34).

At A, on the extreme left, there is a painting which, my informants agreed, was a representation of the lizard-man, Linga, who killed and ate the young Kunia girl (p.126). At B, immediately above, and at I and O, are "tree-like" designs; at C, D, J, K, R and T, simple concentric circles; and on the left-hand side of G, an interesting group of human footprints.

In the middle of a large group of concentric circles, H, is the painting of an aboriginal whose blood, pouring from his arm,[6] has formed a pool at his feet (see figure at X, with the circles eliminated). E is a human figure the head of which has disappeared; F, probably the lower part of a lizard; and G, a man wearing a ceremonial head-dress, called a *nuiti*, which surrounds the face (Pl. 106B). L is a string cross or *wanigi*, which a performer carries on his back during a ceremony (Pl. 106C); N, a goanna associated with a number of conventionalized footprints; and M, P, and S, motifs which almost certainly represent a ceremonial pole, with feathers at the top, called *nurtunja* by the Aranda tribe[7] (Pl. 106A).

Figure 32. Inside the same cave, opposite the main gallery, there is another group of paintings. E, F, G, and H are the modified "tree" designs, mentioned earlier, the latter having radiating lines at the

[6] Adult aborigines, by opening a vein in their arm and allowing the blood to fall into a wooden dish or on the body of one of the performers in a ceremony, provide an adhesive that will hold the coloured plant down or feather decorations in place.

[7] Spencer and Gillen (1899, Figs 53, 68, 81, 88, etc.) describe and illustrate many examples of this ceremonial object, called *waninga* by the Aranda.

A

PLATE 106. Ceremonial decorations of the Pitjandjara: A, Nurtunja pole; B, Head ornament, nuiti; C, String ornament, wanigi.

B

C

top resembling those on the *nurtunja* designs on the opposite wall (Fig. 34M, P and S).

There is also a series of faded complex designs in red and white on the wall of a low opening between two large boulders at the front of the main cave. At D are two "tree" designs; A is a similar isolated design, and B and C, abstract incomprehensible figures.

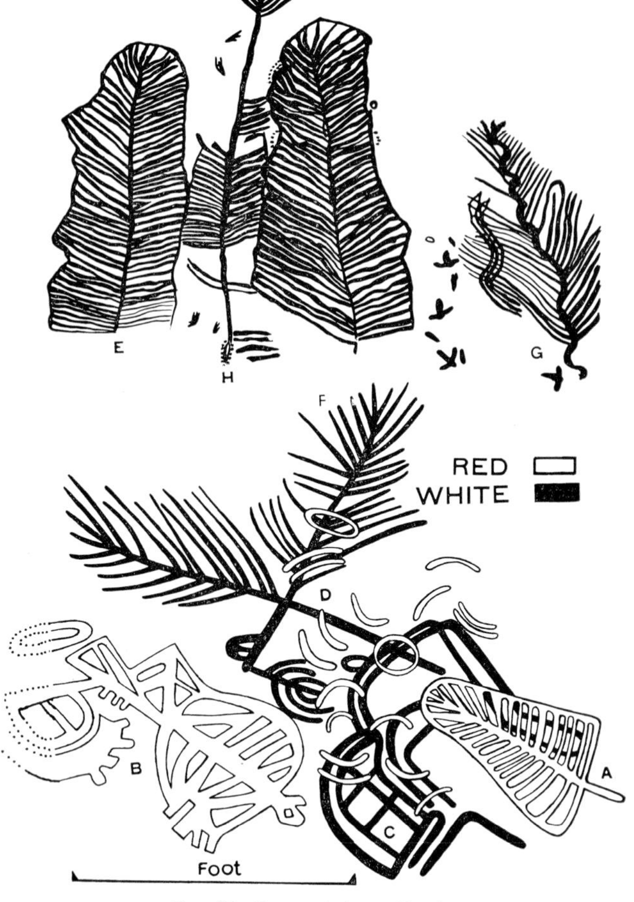

Fig. 32. Cave paintings, Site 4.

There are also crescent-like designs of unknown meaning interspersed throughout the lower panel.

Site 5

This is a shallow cave (Plates 17A, 97B) in the face of a large isolated boulder adjacent to the place where the mythical carpet-snake woman, Bulari, gave birth to a child (Pl. 15A and Fig. 3).

Figure 33. The major design A, B, C, represents an emu hunt by the sleepy-lizard man, Meta-lungana. This painting has been fully described on p.144. D represents a white man shooting a kangaroo;[8]

[8] The white man is always depicted with a hat on his head (see Mountford, 1955, pp. 545-52, Fig. 3), also Figs M, R, S in the initiation cave (Site 9).

E, an aboriginal wearing a circular head-dress, *nuiti* (Pl. 106B); F, a series of paintings illustrating an aboriginal tracking a kangaroo: and G, a simple "tree" and snake design.

Painting H, found in the cave of Minma Kadidi (Pl. 90A and Fig. 3), is a simple representation of an emu hunt. The hunter has cast a spear at an emu, which has escaped, dragging the spear alongside (full lines beside the bird-tracks). The patch of white paint at the top symbolizes where the hunter (indicated by the line of human footprints) caught and killed the emu.

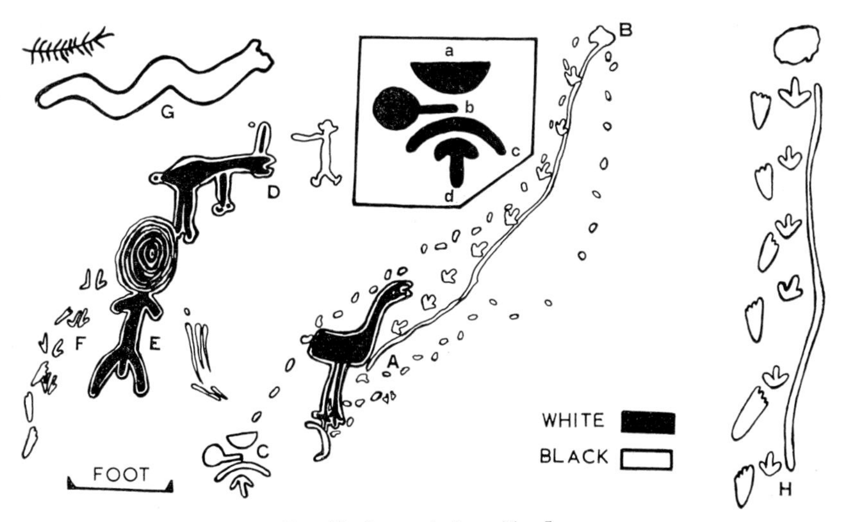

FIG. 33. Cave paintings, Site 5.

Site 6

Site 6 is a cave on the western side of Ayers Rock, which, according to the mythical stories, was once a wet-weather shelter of the marsupial-moles, Itjari-tjari (Pl. 85B and Fig. 3). The back wall of this cave which, being low with an overhanging roof, is an excellent camping place, is covered with a maze of designs, many of which are incomplete, while others are so faint that it is difficult to follow their outlines.

Figure 35. There are two groups of concentric circles at A; a number of unidentified bird tracks and those of an emu seated on the ground at B; an incomplete lizard design at C; a badly weathered complex pattern (similar to Fig. 40D), which one of my informants suggested was a representation of a body decoration, at D; and a painting at E which could represent a pubic tassel on a string. There are a number of "tree" designs, at G, H, L, M, O, R and S; *nurtunja* patterns at J, K, U, Y; remnants of the upper part of human figures with outstretched arms at I (similar to Figs 30D, E and F at Site 2). A long meandering line at V, V, V, almost certainly represents a snake. The paintings at F, Q, N and X are indecipherable. Two of a number of much-defaced paintings on the outer overhang of the cave are recorded in Fig. 43; B could represent a ceremonial head-dress; there is no explanation for E.

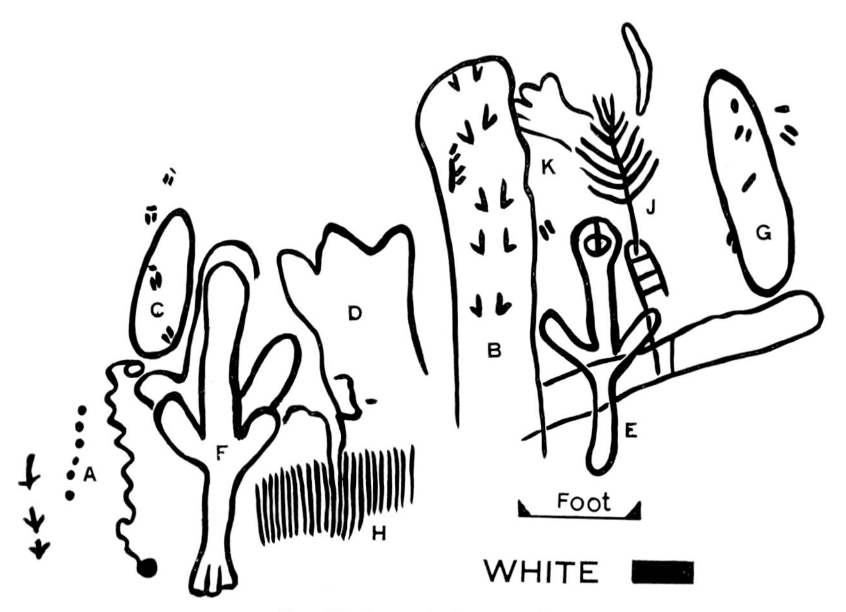

FIG. 37. Cave paintings, Site 7.

Site 7

A number of cylindrical caves north of Site 6 have been eroded almost to ground level. The aborigines have painted a small group of designs in the most southerly of them.

Figure 37. At A, on the extreme left-hand corner, there is a series of bird tracks, a line of dots and a meandering line which probably represents the track of a snake; F and E bear some resemblance to the footmarks of an emu seated on the ground; and D, to an incomplete human figure with up-stretched arms. B is part of a rectangle enclosing a line of paired kangaroo tracks; C and G, oval designs possibly representing *kulpidji*; J a "tree-like" painting; and

K, a crudely painted hand. There is no information about H, which may represent a series of tally marks.[9]

Site 8 (Upper)

Two separate groups of cave paintings were found at this site, one group in the upper, long cylindrical cave (similar to Site 7), and another in a cave with a small opening at ground level.

Figure 38 (upper cave). Fig. 38A, C, are probably representations of *nurtunja* poles (Pl. 106A), with bunches of feathers at the top. The aborigines explained that B is a *kulpidji*, the radiating lines on the edge symbolizing the bird-down with which it is decorated. There are a number of human footprints, bird tracks and indecipherable designs scattered over the cave. The inset illustrates four groups of concentric circles linked with parallel lines.

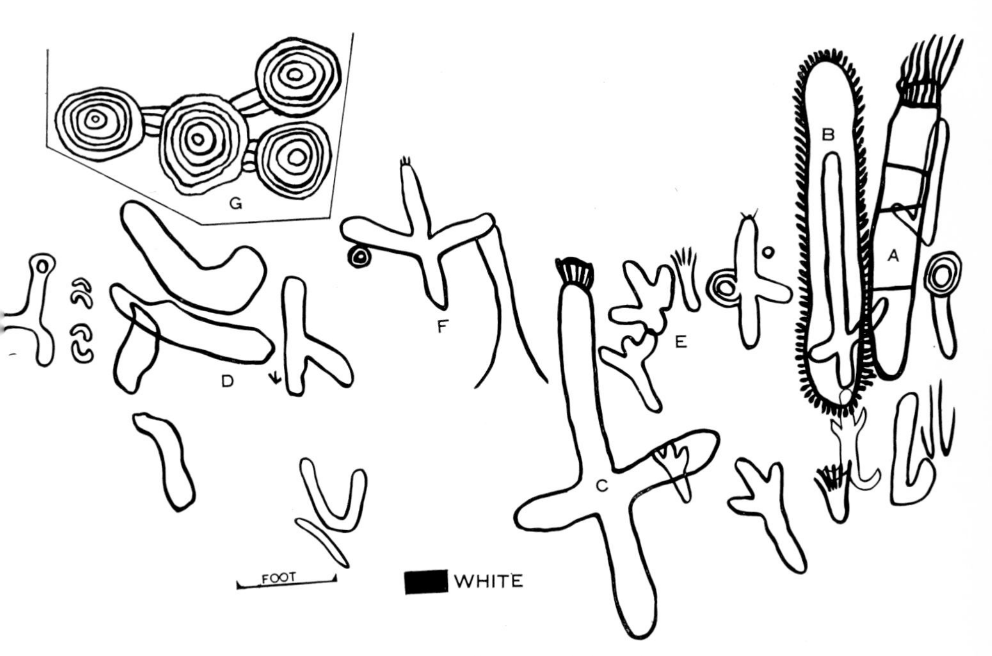

Fig. 38. Cave paintings, Site 8 (upper).

Site 8 (Lower)

In the lower cave, formed by a huge boulder which has slipped from the side of Ayers Rock, there is a wide range of interesting figures. It is unfortunate, however, that owing to overpainting and

[9] The writer has seen and photographed the desert aborigines drawing similar marks in the sand to indicate a sequence of events, such as the number of days spent on a journey.

the smoke from the camp fires it was not possible to distinguish, with any degree of certainty, more than a small proportion of these paintings. These will be described in two groups, i.e. Figs 39 and 40.

Figure 39. According to the aborigines, A represents a ceremonial object similar to a *kulpidji* which has been decorated with bird-down (indicated by the radiating lines along the periphery). B is the painting of a bird which, although clearly visible in 1940, has now entirely disappeared; C, a complex, undecipherable design in red;

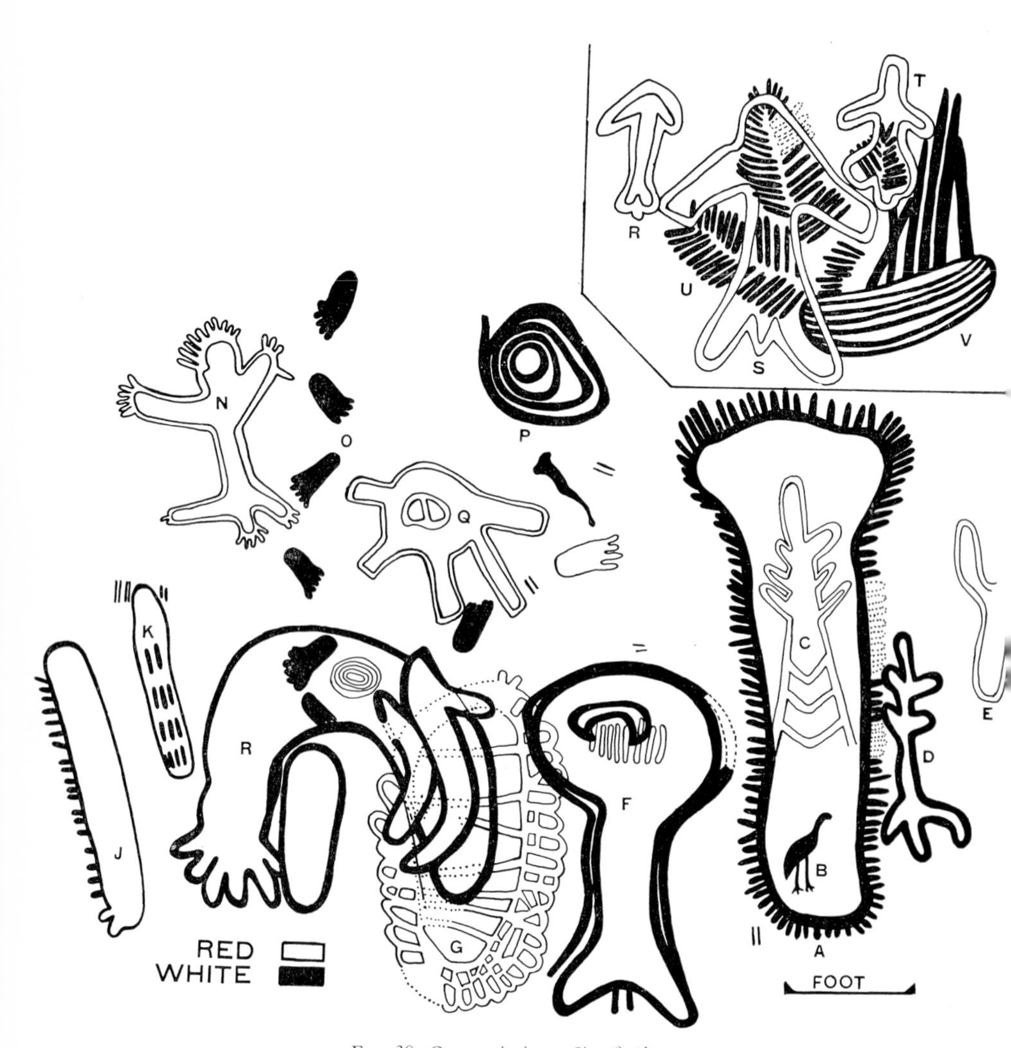

FIG. 39. Cave paintings, Site 8 (lower).

D, possibly a badly executed human figure; E, an incomplete meandering design; R is a large hand and arm; J, K, *kulpidji*-like designs; and N, a human figure in red having projections from its head, arms, legs and penis that resemble Fig. 31N, Site 3. There is a series of concentric circles at P; a line of well-executed human footprints at O, and three complex indecipherable designs at F, G and Q. The inset illustrates a small number of interesting figures on the cave wall above the main group; R, S, T are stylized human figures, R being incomplete; U, an incomplete "tree" design; and V, a design that cannot be identified.

Figure 40. The aborigines explained that the main design, A, represents the spirit dingo, Kulpunya, who travelled from Kikingura to punish the hare-wallaby people at Ayers Rock (p.108). Behind him, leading to the right, B and C, is a line of twelve of his footprints. Spencer and Gillen (1899, Fig. 124) figured this painting and also some of the dingo tracks. Stirling, who made the sketch, not associating these tracks with the dingo design and misled by a fortuitous spot

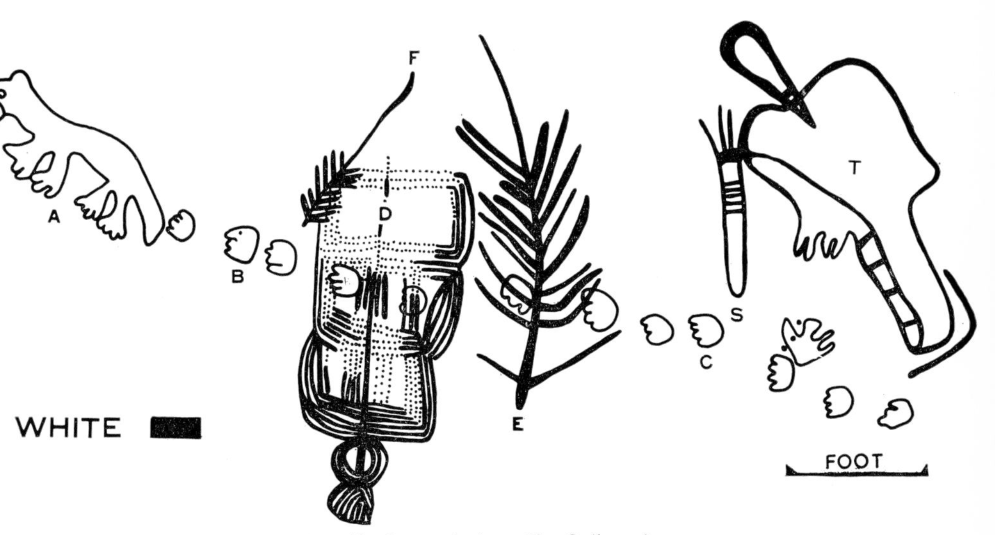

FIG. 40. Cave paintings, Site 8 (lower).

of white paint on one of them (B, Fig. 40), identified them as human faces. E and F are "tree" designs; S, a *nurtunja* with feathers at the top (similar to M, P, S, Fig. 34); and D, a design which, the aborigines explained, was the representation of a ceremonial body decoration (see D, Fig. 35).

Site 9

This site is a long cylindrical cave (Pl. 58A and Fig. 3) in which the Pitjandjara youths passed through the rites of circumcision and sub-incision. As this place has never been a common camping ground, the women being rigidly excluded, the cave is not crowded with paintings—as at Mutitjilda (Site 2), or in the cave of the marsupial mole (Site 6)—the back wall, about ninety feet long, being decorated only with a single line of interesting figures.

In this cave there is strong evidence that the secular art of the aborigines, being unrestricted by ceremonial taboos (such as on the *kulpidji*), tends to keep up-to-date; for, alongside sacred objects (Fig. 36F, and W) and men wearing ceremonial head-dresses (Fig. 36V, X and Y), there are paintings of white men (with hats) shooting bullocks or emus, or riding horses (Figs 36H, R and S).

Figure 36. During my first visit to this cave in 1940, Moanya, one of my aboriginal companions, painted a design on the cave wall that dealt with the myth of the fig-tree man of Jirin-jirin, whose totemic place is in the Musgrave Ranges. This gave me the opportunity of watching an aboriginal artist at work, of finding out the meanings of the designs he painted, and the details of the myth he illustrated.

Using his forefinger as a brush, the aboriginal first painted a design, in red, of a male figure, symbolizing the mythical fig-tree man of Jirin-jirin. When the fundamental design was complete, the artist, using a strip of bark chewed at one end, outlined the figure in white.

The completed painting, Fig. 36B, shows a male figure in which the conventional head is replaced by a wide circle with radiating lines projecting from its upper edge. This design, the artist explained, was the *nuiti* (Pl. 106B), worn by the fig-tree man of creation times, and by the actors of the present day when they take part in his rituals.

At Jirin-jirin there are a number of sacred fig-trees (*Ficus platypoda*). At the correct season the men and women perform a ceremony at this place which, they believe, will ensure a plentiful supply of wild figs during the coming season.

To the accompaniment of the chants belonging to the mythical fig-tree man, the men, decorated with the traditional head-dress and body paintings, dance up to the tree and, by shaking the branches, cause the ripe fruit to fall to the ground. The women, with their eyes lowered (under no circumstances must they look at the tree), collect the fruit, put it in their wooden dishes, and carry it to their camp some distance away. After the women have left, the men, opening the veins in their arms, "water" (an aboriginal term) the tree, by allowing their blood to fall on the tree trunks. This ritual, Moanya assured me, would cause the fig-trees "everywhere in the world" to bear much fruit.

Whilst Moanya was painting the design of the fig-tree man of Jirin-jirin, his companion, old Tjalarina, started to paint his own totemic designs near by (Fig. 36L). These designs dealt both with the wallaby (*wara*) increase rituals at Malupidi in the Tomkinson Ranges, and the episode of a mythical uninitiated wallaby youth and the diamond-sparrows.

One painting (Fig. 36CC) which might easily have been interpreted as a "tree", has an entirely different meaning.[10] An uninitiated youth, starting from CC, crept up to spear some mythical diamond-sparrows who were camping behind a windbreak at a. But when he cast his spear the birds escaped and flew to the waterhole, b, where they made another camp. Again the wallaby-youth crept up and cast his spear, this time killing several of the birds, the remainder flying to another waterhole at c. Here the same incidents occurred, the birds flying to d, but this time, when the youth cast his spear, the birds escaped.

The central vertical panel in the painting CC symbolizes the track made by the youth as he crept up to the camps of the diamond-sparrows, and the projections, a, b, c, d, the windbreaks of the camps of the birds.

The line of tracks, DD, refers to the wallaby (*wara*) increase centre at Malupidi. During creation times the mythical wallabies of Malupidi were pursued by the same youth who speared the diamond-sparrows at CC. The wallabies, however, hopping along DD, escaped by entering a cave at EE. This cave has since been transformed into a pile of boulders, and the tracks into depressions in the rocky surface.

During the rituals for the increase of wallabies, the aborigines, suitably decorated and singing the appropriate chants, hop from one track to the other until they reach the pile of boulders at EE, just as the mythical wallabies did in the long distant past. On arrival, the men rub red ochre over the boulders believing that this ritual will prevent the wallabies from sheltering in deep caves where they cannot be speared by the hunters. At the same time, the actors push green grass among the boulders, a ritual, Tjalarina

[10] This is an excellent example of how it is impossible to interpret, unaided, any painting or engraving made by the desert aborigines. Although I have referred earlier to "tree-like" designs as a matter of convenience, this design shows that, on occasions, some of them would have totally different meanings.

explained, to ensure that there would be so much grass about for the wallabies that they would become fat and lazy.

Both artists assured me that the paintings they had made were without magical value. They had been painted to illustrate the myths of the fig-tree totemic place of Jirin-jirin and of the wallaby centre of Malupidi.

There is no first-hand information available for the remainder of the paintings in the initiation cave. The badly drawn figure, Fig. 36A, could represent either a kangaroo or a dingo. D is a kangaroo; G, an emu; J, a highly conventionalized bird; H, a white man[11] shooting a bullock; R, another emu; and S, another white man riding a horse.[12]

There are human figures at C, N, O, T, U, Z; a man and a woman at Q; others at V, X and Y are wearing ceremonial head-dresses. F is possibly a *kulpidji*; and E, a series of "tree-like" designs. K and M are conventionalized human figures with upstretched arms similar to Fig. 30D, E, and F (Site 2); and W, probably a *kulpidji* with engraved designs on its surface.

The paintings in Fig. 43A and F were found on the surface of a

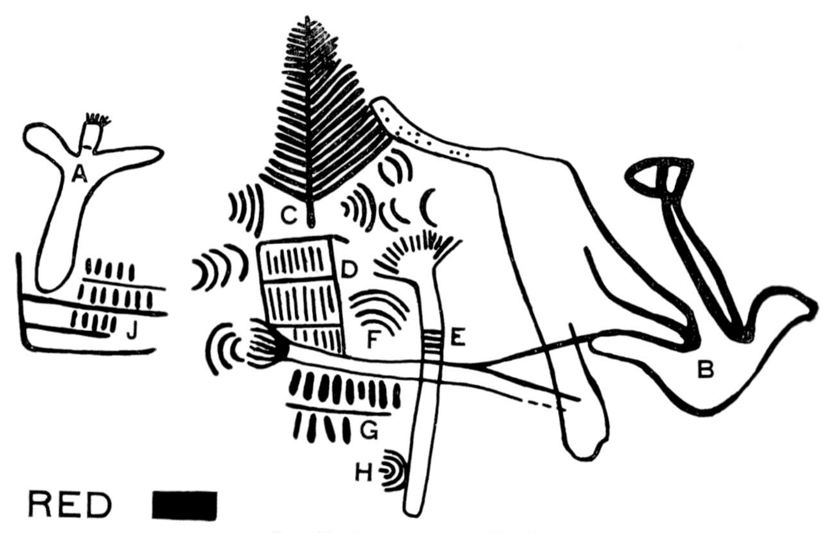

FIG. 41. Cave paintings, Site 11.

split boulder (Pl. 60A) on the plain at the base of the initiation cave (Pl. 58A). A bears some resemblance to a *kulpidji* design, and F is a painting of an aboriginal man.

[11] The white man, as mentioned previously (p.184n), is shown wearing a hat. This is evident in Figs H, R and S. It is also probable that O and Q have similar meanings.

[12] The aboriginal artist, unable to draw a horse, turned a kangaroo over on its four legs and placed the man on top. This is indicated by the long ears and thick tail of the "horse".

Site 10

The tumbled boulders at the base of the camps of the hare-wallaby (Mala) women (Pls 33, 34 and Fig. 3) have sometimes formed themselves into small caves in which there are a few heavily eroded cave paintings.

Figure 43. Two of the cave paintings from this site are shown in Fig. 43. D illustrates two human figures joined together by a series of parallel lines; and C, an incomplete design resembling a *kulpidji*.

Site 11

In one of the shallow caves associated with the kingfisher-woman, Lunba (Fig. 3), there is a group of paintings so faint that it was difficult to unravel the designs.

Figure 41. The painting A probably represents a tribesman wearing a ceremonial head-dress; B, an indecipherable symbol; C, a "tree" design; D, G and J, groups of parallel lines, about which there is no data; E and F, two *nurtunja* poles (Pl. 106A); and H, the grouped crescents so common on the art of the sacred objects.

Site 12

The paintings shown in Fig 42 are in a cave (Pl. 45A and Fig. 3) which was once the camp of the old Mala (hare-wallaby) man, whose duty it was to keep watch on the hare-wallaby women at Tabudja, a low hill a few hundred yards to the north (Fig. 3). A, B and C are the well-known human figures wearing ceremonial head-dresses; D, possibly a lizard; and G, a snake. There is no explanation for the meandering lines J, nor the designs at E.

In the group of designs to the left, K is a pair of human figures, the one on the left wearing some form of head-dress; and P, a series of concentric circles. There are a number of kangaroo feet and tail marks at O and indecipherable figures at L, M and N.

FIG. 42. Cave paintings, Site 12.

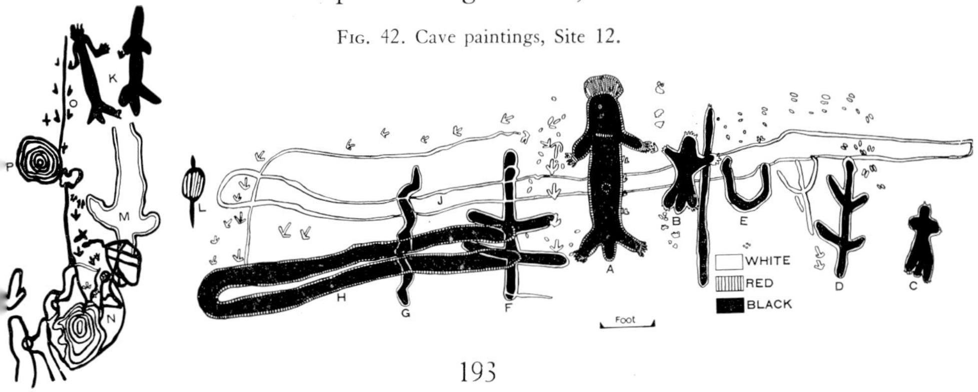

FIG. 43. Cave paintings, Ayers Rock.

SUMMARY

SUMMARY

This study deals with Ayers Rock, a huge monolith in the western desert of central Australia, and the daily life, philosophical beliefs and art forms of its aboriginal inhabitants, the Pitjandjara tribe.

These people possess remarkably few tools, yet this lack of material possessions is balanced by a detailed knowledge of the country in which they live. Both men and women are trained from their earliest childhood to know the sources of food available to them throughout the yearly cycle.

A well-defined area of land is the exclusive property of a family group, within the boundaries of which they normally gain a livelihood. Here, the men hunt the large creatures, kangaroos, wallabies and emus, while the women travel in a more direct route from one waterhole to the next, collecting the grass-seeds, fruits and small creatures on the way. The Pitjandjara have evolved a system of food distribution in which everyone in the group receives a share, a wise custom in a country where food is often in short supply.

The kindliness, intelligence and remarkable honesty of these aboriginal people have been stressed by many of the early explorers and investigators. This study supports their statements.

An examination of the myths of Ayers Rock reveals how closely its aboriginal inhabitants are bound, philosophically, to their surroundings. Everything that the aborigines see about them, the immense precipices, the deep embayments, the waterholes and the caves that keep them warm in winter and cool in summer are, to them, undeniable evidence of the authenticity of the myths explaining their origin.

One of the first images to reach the mind of an aboriginal child born at Ayers Rock would be the sight of those great rocks and precipices, and one of the first stories told to him would be a simple myth explaining their creation.

With a boy, this knowledge becomes richer as, with the passing years, the tribal elders admit him deeper and deeper into the esoteric mysteries of the tribe until, by the time he is fully adult, Ayers Rock and its myths are the central theme in his life. He belongs to a world completely dominated by the natural features surrounding him. It is a small world, but his knowledge of it is deep and strong. The young tribesman feels he is one of a continuous line of progenitors uniting him with the great *tjukurapa* creatures of the dim and ghostly past. They, his own forbears, brought into existence everything with which he is in daily contact; the monolith of Uluru, the cycle of the seasons, the pattern of his daily life, the ceremonial life, and the code of laws under which he lives.

Most aspects of the daily and ceremonial life are reflected in the local topography: the social organization of the tribe by the sharp division of the base of the monolith into the territories of the *Nananduraḳa* and *Tanamildjan* moieties; the ceremonial life by the initiation cave of the hare-wallaby people; the beliefs of the spirit world by the children of Tjinderi-tjinderiba who still search for earthly mothers; the magical ritual by which the aborigines believe they can control the rhythm of Nature through the increase stones of the mythical carpet-snakes and the sleepy-lizard, and the power of *aruḳwita*, that deadly essence of disease and death symbolized by the white marks in the cave of the mourning carpet-snake woman.

The aborigines personify the physical features of their environment to a degree which we, trained in a European tradition, find it difficult to understand. To us, Ayers Rock is a huge monolith of vertically bedded arkose of uncertain age; to the aborigines, it is living evidence of the deeds of their *tjuḳurapa* heroes of the long-distant past. Mutitjilda, on the southern face is not, according to the ancient stories, filled with water, but with the transformed blood of the dying carpet-snake man; the grey patch on the southern cliff of Uluru is not an extensive patch of lichen, but the metamorphosed smoke from the burning camp of the greedy sleepy-lizard; and the huge semi-detached column of rock on the north-westerly corner is not an unusual example of exfoliation, but the transformed ritual pole that once stood in the centre of the initiation ground of the hare-wallaby men.

At the same time the physical environment reflects episodes in the mythical stories which show the widely varying temperaments of the totemic heroes of *tjuḳurapa* times, for the aborigines do not believe in a Golden Age when all was perfect. Their mythical forbears were both good and bad, just as men are today.

These episodes tell of the harmless carpet-snakes who lived peaceably on the eastern end of Uluru until they were attacked and destroyed by the trouble-making and belligerent poisonous snakes; the angry mother of the dying carpet-snake man and her quick revenge; the quarrel between the hare-wallabies and the mulga-seed tribesmen of Kikingura, and the killing of so many of them by the spirit dingo, Kulpunya; the useless murder of Tjinderi-tjinderiba, the mother of the tiny spirit children, and the destruction of the sleepy-lizard man because of his meanness.

These stories of the mythical past are expressed in all forms of the aborigines' cultural outlets. They are the core of their ceremonial life, the theme of their ritualistic songs, and the subject of their art. It is through these media that the aborigines of Ayers Rock keep alive the ties that bind them so closely to Uluru, the great monolith under whose shadow they were born.

The art of Ayers Rock, one of the cultural outlets by which the aborigines transmit these mythical beliefs from one generation to the next, is among the simplest of any living people. It consists of three distinct forms:

(*a*) Indentations in the rock surface, an ancient art which the aborigines claim is not the work of their kind, but of one or another of the mythical beings of creation times. These rock engravings may be examples of man's first strivings to express himself in graphical form.

(*b*) Engravings on the sacred objects, the *ḳulpidji*, one of the means by which the aborigines, using a particularly limited symbolism, preserve the esoteric history of the tribe.

(*c*) Paintings in the caves, where the artist, unrestricted by the taboos of the ritualistic life, is able to use a much wider range of motifs than on the *ḳulpidji*. This living art tends to keep up to date, for beside simple abstract designs there are paintings of white men shooting bullocks, kangaroos and emus, or riding horses.

Most of the paintings in the caves of Ayers Rock, although incomprehensible to the white man, would be full of rich significance to the aborigines who produced them.

It was possible to glimpse this richness, although but dimly, from the fragmentary accounts given by the artists, Moanya and Tjalarina, as they described the increase rituals of the fig-tree man of Jirin-jirin and those of the wallaby people of Malupidi. There was no doubt that, as these men painted their simple pictures on the cave wall, they visualized the rituals with which those paintings were associated, the atmosphere of the ceremonial ground with its circles of chanting men, and the dancers and actors with their colourful body decorations. Behind all of these mental images, like a backdrop, would be the knowledge of the mythical stories explaining the origin of everything in the world of the aborigines.

This study also reveals that, at Ayers Rock, in the arid centre of a continent on the edge of the world, communities of stone-age food-gathering and hunting people are still practising an art comparable to that of paleolithic man who lived in Europe so many thousands of years ago.

BIBLIOGRAPHY

BASEDOW, H. (1914), Aboriginal Rock Carvings of Great Antiquity in South Australia: *Journ. Roy. Anthrop. Inst.*, vol. 44, pp. 195-211.

ELKIN, A. P. (1939), Kinship in South Australia: *Oceania*, vol. 10, pp. 198-234.

EYRE, E. J. (1845), *Journals of Expeditions of Discovery into Central Australia, and Overland from Adelaide to King George's Sound in the years 1840-41, including an account of the manners and customs of the Aborigines.* Vol. 2. London.

FINLAYSON, H. H. (1935), *The Red Centre.* Sydney.

FRY, H. K. (1935), Aboriginal Mentality: *Med. Journ. Aust.*, vol. 1, no. 12.

GREY, G. (1841), *Journals of Two Expeditions of Discovery in North-west and Western Australia.* 2 vols. London.

GREGORY, J. W. (1906), *The Dead Heart of Australia.* London.

HARNEY, W. E. (1960), Ritual and Behaviour at Ayers Rock: *Oceania*, vol. 21, no. 1.

LOVE, J. R. B. (1943), A Primitive Method of Making a Wooden Dish by Native Women of the Musgrave Ranges of South Australia: *Trans. Roy. Soc. S. Aust.*, vol. 66, pp. 215-17.

McCARTHY, F. D., and MACINTOSH, N. W. G. (1962), Archaeology of Mootwingee, Western New South Wales: *Rec. Aust. Museum*, vol. 25, pp. 249-98.

MOUNTFORD, C. P. (1928), Aboriginal Rock Carvings in South Australia: *Assoc. Adv. Sci.*, Hobart, pp. 337-66.

——— (1929), A Unique Example of Aboriginal Rock Carving at Panaramitee North: *Trans. Roy. Soc. S. Aust.*, vol. 53, pp. 245-8.

——— (1937), Rock Paintings at Windulda, Western Australia: *Oceania*, vol. 7, no. 4, pp. 429-35.

——— (1937A), Aboriginal Crayon Drawings . . . of the Northern Aranda Tribe of Central Australia: *Trans. Roy. Soc. S. Aust.*, vol. 61, pp. 84-95.

——— (1938), Aboriginal Crayon Drawings . . . of Wati Kutjara: *Rec. S. Aust. Mus.*, vol. 6, no. 1, pp. 4-28.

——— (1948), *Brown Men and Red Sand.* Melbourne.

——— (1955), An Unrecorded Method of Aboriginal Rock Marking: *Rec. S. Aust. Mus.*, vol. 11, no. 4, pp. 345-52.

——— (1956), *The Art, Myth and Symbolism of Arnhem Land.* Melbourne.

——— (1958), *The Tiwi, Their Art, Myth and Ceremony.* London.

——— (1960), Simple Rock Engravings in Central Australia: *Man*, vol. 60. Article 192.

——— (1962), Rock Engravings at Koonawarra, N.S.W.: *Rec. S. Aust. Museum*, vol. 14, no. 2, pp. 245-8.

——— (1962A), Sacred Objects of the Pitjandjara Tribe, Western Central Australia: *Rec. S. Aust. Museum*, vol. 14, no. 2, pp. 397-411.

MOUNTFORD, C. P., and EDWARDS, R. (1962B), Rock Engravings of Extinct Creatures in South Australia: B: *Man*, vol. 62, Article 174.

MOUNTFORD, C. P., and EDWARDS, R. (1963), Rock Engravings of Panaramitee station, South Australia: *Trans. Roy. Soc. S. Aust.*, vol. 86, pp. 131-46.

MOUNTFORD, C. P., and ROBERTS, A. (n.d.), *Your Guide to the Olgas.* Adelaide.

OLLIER, C. D., and TUDDENHAM, W. F. (1962), Inselbergs of Central Australia: *Zeitshr. f. Geomorph.*, vol. 5, pp. 257-76.

PRINGLE, L. A. B., and KOLLOSCHE, H. E. (1958), Preliminary Notes on Aboriginal Paintings, Carved Stones, Arranged Stones and Stone Structures in the Mount Olga Region of Central Australia: *Trans. Roy. Soc. S. Aust.*, vol. 81, pp. 131-40.

SPENCER, B., and GILLEN, F. (1899), *Native Tribes of Central Australia.* London.

STANNER, W. H. (1956), The Dreaming: *The Australian Signpost*, pp. 51-65.

——— (1961), On Aboriginal Religion. IV, The Design Plan of a Mythless Rite: *Oceania*, vol. 31, pp. 233-58.

TINDALE, N. B. (1935), Initiation among the Pitjandjara Natives of the Mann and Tomkinson Ranges: *Oceania*, vol. 6, pp. 199-224.

INDEX

Aborigines, desert, 4, 5, 10, 13, 24, 187*n*, 191*n*; and honey-ants, 120; attitude to willy-wagtail, 152; attitude to wanambi, 154; of Central Australia, 157, 159; chants of, 174, 190, 191, 199; art of, 176, 190
Adnyamatana tribe, and willy-wagtail, 152
Alabina, honey-ant totem of, 178
Amadeus, Lake, 3
Amphibolurus reticulatus, 120*n*
Aranda tribe, 86, 173, 182*n*
Arnhem Land, western, 175
Art, of Ayers Rock, 155, 199; rock engravings, 157-61, 199; sacred objects, 162-74, 199; cave paintings, 175-94, 199
Arukwita, spirit of disease and death, 32, 50, 54, 56, 60, 96*n*, 177-8, 198
Aspidites ramsayi. See Woma
Ayers Rock (Uluru), geographic position, xiii; clan territories of, 18, 32; myths of, 20, 31-154, 197; topography of, 27-30, 198; aboriginal name for, 30; totems of, 32; northern face of, 84; wanambi at, 154; art of, 155; rock engravings, 157-61; sacred objects, 162-74; cave paintings, 175-94; aborigines of, 197-9

Balinga, xiv, 18, 54, 60, 68*n*, 96, 114, 148, 154
Basedow, H., 158
Basedow Ranges, 3
Bellbird, mythical. *See* Panpanpanala
Bone-pointing, 60
Boomerangs, 10; hooked, 12; Kandju, 114, 119, 120, 169-70
Boulders, Mala, 83, 85, 164-5, 167; Kandju, 117, 118, 120; Linga, 122, 126, 127; Kunia, 126, 127, 128, 163; Itjari-tjari, 131, 132; Kadidi, 132, 136, 137; Meta-lungana, 141, 142, 143, 144, 171; Tjinderi-tjinderiba, 146, 148, 149, 151, 153
Bulari, myth of, 32, 40, 47, 144; carrying dish of, 45; totemic place of, 45; vagina of, 46; cave of, 50, 184
Burra, 157

Cakes, grass-seed, 16
Carpet-snake. *See* Kunia
Carrying bag, 11
Carrying dish, wooden, 8, 11; Itjari-tjari women, 131, 132; Kadidi, 132, 136
Cave paintings, Mala, 97; Meta-lungana, 143, 144; rate of change, 175-6; age of, 176; recording, 176; significance of, 176; techniques of, 177; description of: Site 1, 177-8, 180; Site 2, 178-81; Site 3, 181-2; Site 4, 182-4; Site 5, 184-5; Site 6, 185-6; Site 7, 186-7; Site 8, 187-9; Site 9, 190-2; Site 10, 193; Site 11, 192, 193; Site 12, 193; designs of, 194, 199
Caves, of Ayers Rock, 38, 40, 199; of Bulari, 40, 47, 50, 184; Kunia Ingridi, 55, 60, 97, 177-8; Mala, 78, 82, 85, 167, 193; initiation, 96, 98, 99, 102, 103, 190-2; Lunba, 108, 193; Kandju, 116, 117, 120; Linga, 126; Itjari-tjari, 131, 132, 133-4, 171, 185; Kadidi, 132, 135-6, 185; Meta-lungana, 138, 140, 144, 171-2; Tjinderi-tjinderiba, 148, 153
Central Australia, rock engraving designs, 160-1; art motif of, 172
Ceremonies, increase, 62, 144, 190-2, 198; circumcision, 86, 96

Children, spirit, 31, 152; Mala, 68; Tjinderi-tjinderiba, 148-9, 151-2, 153
Circumcision, of Mala, 86, 96
Clan territories, of Ayers Rock, 18, 32
Conner, Mount, 27, 120*n*
Creation beliefs. *See* Tjukurapa times
Crocodile, salt-water, 158
Crocodilus porosus. *See* Crocodile, salt-water
Cutting tools, 7, 10-11

Davidson, —, 173
Death, spirit of. *See* Arukwita
Decorations, ceremonial. *See* Nuiti and Wanigi
Designs, sacred object, 159-74
Diamond-sparrows, mythical, 191
Digging stick, wooden, 8, 11
Dingo, spirit. *See* Kulpunya
Disease, spirit of. *See* Arukwita

Eagle-chick. *See* Kudrun
Edwards, R., 157, 158, 160
Elkin, A. P., 19*n*
Emus, killed by Meta-lungana, 137, 139, 141, 144; cave painting of, 184, 185; sacred-object design, 171
Eucola, rock engravings at, 158
Euro, hunting of, 14
Ewaninga, rock engravings at, 161
Eyre, E. J., quoted, 4

Ficus platypoda. *See* Fig-tree
Fighting stick, Pitjandjara, 12
Fig-tree, increase ceremony, 190-1
Finlayson, H. H., 15*n*
Firemaking, 8
Flinders Ranges, 152
Food, preparation of, 15-16; distribution of, 17
Food-gathering, equipment for, 7-12; cycle of, 13; skill of, 14; by women, 15-17; by men, 16-17
Fry, H. K., quoted, 5

Gillen, F., 10, 12, 25*n*, 50*n*, 60*n*, 86, 120*n*, 182*n*, 189
Glen Helen, 20
Government, of Pitjandjara tribe, 19-20
Gregory, J. W., quoted, 4
Grey, G., quoted, 5
Grinding stones, 8, 9, 12

Hare-wallabies. *See* Mala
Honey-ants, 120, 121, 126
Hunting, equipment for, 7-12; methods of, 14-15

Increase ritual, Kunia, 62, 198; Meta-lungana, 144, 198; fig-tree, 190-1; wallaby, 191-2
Initiates, Mala, 78, 79, 84-5, 87-8, 89, 90, 91, 96, 99, 102, 114, 165
Initiation cave, 86, 96, 190-2
Initiation ceremony, Mala, 78, 86, 92, 96, 100, 102, 114; sacred-object designs, 165, 166, 167, 174
Iromba, rock engravings at, 160
Itjari-tjari (marsupial mole), myth of, 20, 32, 126, 129-32, 133-4; women, 134; totemic place of, 170, 185; sacred-object designs, 170-1

Jabiaba, aboriginal guide, 5
Jili (fig-trees), 163
Jirin-jirin, fig-tree man of, 190-1, 199
Junabidi, 126

Kadidi (man and woman), 20, 31, 32, 132, 135-6, 138, 185
Kadu rockhole, 170
Kalaia-tjunda rockhole, 32, 137, 138, 171
Kamanalda, aboriginal guide, 5
Kandju (lizard-man), myth of, 27, 31, 114-20; sacred-object designs, 169-70. *See also* Linga
Kandju gorge, 120, 132
Kandju soak, 32, 120, 170
Kangaroo, red, hunting of, 14-15
Kapi Tjukiki rockhole, 33

Katatjuta (Mount Olga), 33, 40, 41, 42, 68, 157, 158, 159, 160, 161, 163, 164
Kikingura, home of mulga-seed men, 102, 107, 108, 168, 172, 189, 198
Kingfisher woman. *See* Lunba
Kollosche, H. E., 160
Koonawarra, rock engravings at, 158
Korporilya, rock engravings at, 160
Kudrun (eagle-chick), 78, 102, 108; death of, 109, 114; sacred-object design, 169
Kulikudjeri, leader of Liru, 33, 50, 54, 68, 148, 179
Kulpidji (sacred objects), designs, 86, 155, 172-4, 199; Kunia and Liru, 162-4, 167; Mala and Kulpunya, 164-9; Kandju, 169-70; Itjari-tjari, 170-1; Meta-lungana, 171-2; analysis of, 172-4; cave paintings of, 186, 187, 192, 193
Kulpunya (spirit dingo), and Ayers Rock, 31; stopping places of, 32; and Mala, 68; myth of, 102, 104, 107-11, 114; sacred-object designs, 168-9, 173; cave paintings of, 182, 189
Kunduna snakes, 68
Kunia, clan lands of, 18; myth of, 20, 31-68; Ungata, 60, 62, 63; increase rituals of, 62; girl killed by Linga, 124-5, 126, 127-8; and Meta-lungana, 138, 144; sacred-object designs, 162-3
Kunia boulders, 32, 34, 36-7, 57-8, 59, 60, 62, 64. *See also* Boulders
Kunia Ingridi, 32, 50, 54, 55, 59, 60, 61, 64, 68, 96*n*, 97; killing of Kulikudjeri, 148; cave of, 177-8
Kunia men, 32, 38
Kunia rockhole, 32
Kunia women, 32, 35; camps of, 38, 63; dish of, 39; boulders of, 39; sacred-object design, 163
Kuniapiti, camp of Kunia, 32, 60, 62
Kuran (spirit), 154
Kurunba (life essence), 23, 25*n*, 62, 144, 162

Largorchestes hirsutus. *See* Mala
Liasis childreni. *See* Kunia
Liebig, Mount, 68
Life essence. *See* Kurunba
Linga (lizard-man), and Ayers Rock, 31; camp of, 32, 121-3, 126; myth of, 114, 120-6, 127-8; killing of Kunia girl, 126; cave paintings of, 182. *See also* Kandju
Liru (poisonous snakes), and Ayers Rock, 31; myth of, 31-68; leader of, 33, 50, 54, 68, 148, 179; camps of, 41-2, 159; fight with Kunia, 43, 44, 48, 60, 68; rape of Mala woman, 65, 66, 68; killing of Tjinderi-tjinderiba, 146-7, 148; sacred-object designs, 163-4, 167-8
Liru spears, holes of, 44
Liru waterhole, 163
Lizard-men. *See* Kandju and Linga
Love, J. R. B., 8*n*
Lukiri caves, paintings of, 175
Lunba (red-backed kingfisher woman), and Ayers Rock, 31; camps of, 32; myth of, 104-6, 108, 114; sacred object of, 164; cave paintings of, 193
Lurubunangi, ceremony of, 62

McCarthy, F. D., 158
MacDonnell Ranges, 20
Macintosh, N. W. G., 158
Mala, clan lands of, 18; myth of, 20, 67, 68-114; and Ayers Rock, 31; track of, 32, 66; initiates, 32, 78, 84-6, 114, 165; caves, 68, 74; at Tabudja, 74-8; initiation, 78, 86, 96; and Kulpunya, 102-14, 164-9; and Lunba, 104-6, 108, 114; sacred-object designs, 164-9; cave paintings, 193
Mala boulders, 71, 74, 76, 79, 87, 88, 89-91, 94, 95, 98, 100. *See also* Boulders

Mala children, camp of, 68, 69, 70, 74, 75, 77, 80; myth of, 79, 80; sacred-object design, 167
Mala men, old, 32, 74, 78, 86, 87, 88, 90; camps of, 82, 84, 113; chanting, 98; in initiation ceremony, 101; sacred-object designs, 164-5, 167
Mala women, myth of, 32, 65-6, 75, 76; camp of, 67, 68, 74, 79-81, 120, 193; rape of, 68; breasts of, 69, 74, 77; clitoris, 71, 74; digging stick, 73, 74; pubic hairs, 74, 76; sacred-object designs, 166, 167-8, 169
Malupidi, 191, 199
Mann Ranges, 154*n*
Maratjara spring, 31, 33, 162
Marriage, Pitjandjara tribe, 19
Marsupial mole. *See* Itjari-tjari
Marununga, 68
Matinya, aboriginal, 98
Melophorous inflatus. See honey-ants
Meta-lungana (sleepy-lizard), myth of, 20, 32, 137, 138-44; and Ayers Rock, 31; camps of, 138, 140, 171; and Kunia, 138, 144; cave paintings of, 143, 144, 184; increase ritual of, 144, 198; sacred-object designs, 171-2
Metjan gorge, 138, 144
Metjan waterhole, 32, 139, 144
Mimi art, 175
Minma Bulari. *See* Bulari
Minma Kadidi. *See* Kadidi
Moanya, aboriginal guide, 5, 190, 191, 199
Mountford, C. P., 8*n*, 25*n*, 68*n*, 154*n*, 157, 158, 159, 160, 161, 162, 172, 177*n*, 178*n*, 181, 185*n*; field notes, 7, 18*n*, 20*n*, 152*n*, 175*n*
Mulga-seed men, 172, 198. *See also* Windulka
Mulga-trees, 86, 89
Munbun, Pitjandjara man, 154
Musgrave Ranges, 3, 14, 96*n*, 126, 190
Mutitjilda waterhole, 27, 49, 54, 154, 198; gorge, 48, 49, 50, 54, 62, 178; cave paintings, 175-6, 178-81
Myths, Orion and Pleiades, 20; Yarapi, 20; and Ayers Rock, 30, 31; Woma, 31; Kunia and Liru, 31-68, 162-4, 198; Tjinderi-tjinderiba, 68, 144-52, 153, 198; Mala and Kulpunya, 68-114, 164-9, 198; Kandju and Linga, 114-26, 127-8, 169-70; Itjari-tjari, 126, 129-32, 133-4, 170-1; Kadidi, 132, 135-6, 138; Meta-lungana, 137, 138-44, 171-2, 198; wanambi, 152, 154

Naldawata pole, 32, 86, 92-5, 112, 114; sacred-object designs, 166, 173, 174
Nananduraka, tribal group, 19, 68, 69, 96, 152, 198
Native Tribes of Central Australia, 10, 12, 25*n*
Ngadadjara tribe, 96*n*
Ngama, rock engravings at, 160; cave paintings at, 175
Notoryctes typhlops. See Itjari-tjari
Nuiti (head-dress), 183; cave paintings of, 182, 185, 190
Numidi, aboriginal, 5
Nurtunja pole, 86, 183; cave paintings of, 182, 186, 187, 189, 193

Olga, Mount, 27. *See also* Katatjuta
Ollier, C. D., 27; quoted, 30
Oolra spring, 114

Panaramitee, rock engravings at, 158, 160
Panpanpanala (bell-bird), 32, 102, 111
Patina, red-brown, 159
Petermann Ranges, 102, 172
Pitjandjara, tribal land of, 3, 197; equipment of, 7-12, 197; food-gathering, 13-17, 197; food distri-

Pitjandjara—*continued*
bution, 17, 197; clan territories of, 18, 197; social structure of, 19, 68, 96, 198; government of, 19-20; beliefs of, 23-6, 197; universe of, 24-6; attitude to willy-wagtail, 152; art motifs, 155, 172, 174, 176, 178; rock engravings, 157-61, 199; sacred objects, 162-74, 199; cave paintings, 175-94, 199; circumcision rites of, 190
Pitjandjara myths, 20, 197-9; Kunia and Liru, 31-68; Mala and Kulpunya, 68-114; Kandju and Linga, 114-26, 127-8; Itjari-tjari, 126, 129-32, 133-4; Kadidi, 132, 135-6, 138; Meta-lungana, 137, 138-44; Tjinderi-tjinderiba, 144-52, 153; wanambi, 152, 154
Pringle, L. A. B., 160
Pugabuga, snakes of, 31
Pungalunga men, 68

Rainbow serpent. *See* Wanambi
Rawlinson Ranges, 3
Rhipidura leucophrys. *See* Tjinderi-tjinderiba
Roberts, A., 160
Rock engravings, distribution of, 157; origin of, 157, 199; age of, 157-8; motifs of, 158; techniques used, 158-9; description of, 159-61
Rock-markings, scars of Tjinderi-tjinderiba, 145

Sacred objects. *See* Kulpidji
Sahara desert, rock engravings, 161
Sand-lizard. *See* Kandju and Linga
Sheard, L. E., 176, 179
Shield, Pitjandjara, 12
Sir Henry, Mount, 114
Sleepy-lizard. *See* Meta-lungana
Snakes, venomous (*see* Liru); non-venomous (*see* Kunia, Pugabuga, Woma, Wanambi)
Solanum, yellow-fruited. *See* Yirtumba
Spears, hunting, 7, 10; Liru, 32; Kandju, 120
Spearthrowers, 7-8, 10; Kandju, 117, 120; Mala, 91
Spencer, B., 10, 12, 25*n*, 50*n*, 60*n*, 86, 120*n*, 182*n*, 189
Spirit children, of Tjinderi-tjinderiba, 148-9, 151-2, 153. *See also* Yulanya
Spirit dingo. *See* Kulpunya
Stanner, W. H., 23*n*
Strehlow, T. G. H., 25*n*
Sub-incision, ceremony of, 86, 96

Tabuda, 120*n*
Tabudja, camp of Mala, 18, 32, 72-3, 74-7, 78, 79-81, 108, 114, 120, 166-7, 193
Tanamildjan, tribal group, 19, 67, 68, 96, 152, 198
Terry, Michael, 175, 179
Tiliqua scincoides. *See* Meta-lungana
Tindale, N. B., 19*n*, 96*n*
Tiyin rockhole, 159
Tjalarina, 97, 191-2, 199
Tjinderi-tjinderiba (willy-wagtail woman), and Ayers Rock, 31; myth of, 32, 108, 110, 114, 144-52; death of, 68, 148; and Liru, 146-7, 148; children of, 148-9, 151-2, 153; pubic hairs of, 150; rock engravings near, 159
Tjinindi rockhole, 32, 78, 110, 111, 114, 145, 148, 165, 169
Tjukiki gorge, 32, 33, 35, 39, 152, 163
Tjukurapa (creation) times, meaning of, 23; heroes, 25-6, 197-8; and Kunia, 33, 40; circumcision in, 86; Itjari-tjari during, 132; Meta-lungana during, 138; and Tjinderi-tjinderiba, 148; totemic beings of, 154, 157; wanambi of, 154
Tomkinson Ranges, 68, 191
Tools, of Pitjandjara, 7-12, 197

Totemic creatures, of Ayers Rock, 32
Tuddenham, W. F., 27; quoted, 28
Turtle, sea-going, 158

Uluru, home of wanambi, 32, 154. *See also* Ayers Rock
Uluru waterhole, 32, 33, 43, 60, 154, 163

Walbiri tribe, 175
Wallabies, increase ritual, 191-2, 199
Walpa gorge, 160, 161
Wanambi, myth of, 152, 154
Wanigi, string cross, 182, 183
Warburton Ranges, 20, 96*n*
Watelbring waterhole, rock engravings at, 160
Wati Jula, mythical man, 132, 181
Willy-wagtail, taboos associated with, 152
Willy-wagtail woman. *See* Tjinderi-tjinderiba
Wina rockhole, 160
Windulka (mulga-seed) men, 102, 108, 168
Woma, non-venomous snake, 31-2
Wongona grass, 16

X-ray art, 175

Yarapi, myth of, 20, 175
Yirtumba (yellow-fruited solanum), 74, 166
Yulanya (spirit children), 31, 152, 153
Yunta, 158

Zeil, Mount, 178

Mountford - Ayers Rock